SUCCESS RULES

RULES

—— OF ——

BILLIONAIRES

IN THEIR OWN WORDS

Warren Buffet - Mukesh Ambani - Jeff Bezos - Jack Ma - Elon Musk

Aliko Dangote - Bill Gates - Tyler Perry - Oprah Winfrey

Carlos Slim Helu - Robert F. Smith

EDITED BY: FRANCIS E.U.

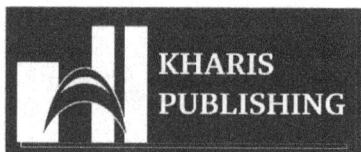
KHARIS PUBLISHING

CONTENTS

Chapter 1

SUCCESS RULES OF WARREN BUFFET

Introduction to Warren Buffett: His life and contributions

Warren Buffett, one of the most successful investors and business magnates of our time, has left an indelible mark on the world of finance, entrepreneurship, and philanthropy. Buffett's journey from humble beginnings to becoming one of the wealthiest individuals on the planet is nothing short of remarkable. This article delves into Buffett's life, contributions to business, investment strategies, and philanthropic endeavors. Through this exploration, we gain insights into the character and principles that have shaped his extraordinary success and enduring influence.

1. Early Life and Entrepreneurial Beginnings

1.1   Childhood and Family Background

Warren Buffett, often referred to as the "Oracle of Omaha," was born on August 30, 1930, in Omaha, Nebraska. He grew up in a middle-class family, the second of three children. His father was a stockbroker and later a congressman, while his mother was a homemaker. Buffett's early exposure to the world of finance and investing came through his father, who would often take him to the stock exchange.

1.2   Education and Academic Years

Buffett demonstrated his entrepreneurial spirit at a young age. As a child, he would buy six-packs of Coca-Cola from his grandfather's grocery store and resell each bottle individually, making a small profit. He also delivered newspapers and worked odd jobs to earn extra money.

Buffett attended Woodrow Wilson High School, where he was known for his keen business sense and exceptional mathematical abilities. He went on to study at the University of Pennsylvania's Wharton School of Business. He transferred to the University of Nebraska-Lincoln due to his dissatisfaction with Wharton's focus on financial institutions rather than investing. He graduated with a Bachelor of Science in business administration and immediately pursued a master's degree in economics from Columbia University, under the guidance of Benjamin Graham (1894–1976), renowned economist and investor who was called "the father of value harvesting."

2. Building a Business Empire: Buffett's Career and Investment Success

2.1 Early Entrepreneurial Ventures

After completing his education, Buffett worked briefly at his father's brokerage firm. In 1956, he formed Buffett Partnership Ltd., his first investment partnership. Over the next decade, Buffett consistently outperformed the market, generating significant returns for his investors.

2.2 Partnership with Berkshire Hathaway

In 1962, Buffett became a majority shareholder in Berkshire Hathaway, a struggling textile manufacturing company. Realizing the textile business was not his forte, he transitioned Berkshire Hathaway into a diversified holding company, focusing on acquiring stock in other businesses. He eventually dissolved the partnerships and used the capital to invest solely in Berkshire Hathaway.

2.3 Notable Investments and Success Stories

Buffett's investment prowess is highlighted by his wise decisions and legendary success stories. Notably, he invested in American Express during a period of financial turmoil and turned it into a highly profitable venture. Buffett also acquired significant stakes in companies like Coca-Cola, Wells Fargo, and IBM, among others, which have yielded substantial returns over the years. Through his disciplined approach and long-term perspective, Buffett has built a business empire that continues to thrive.

3. Investment Philosophy: Principles and Strategies of Warren Buffett

3.1 Value Investing Approach

Buffett is known for his adherence to value investing principles. He seeks out companies whose stock prices are undervalued compared to their intrinsic value. Instead of chasing short-term trends, he focuses on the long-term potential of businesses. Buffett believes in investing in quality companies at reasonable prices, considering them to be undervalued "bargains".

3.2 Long-Term Investment Horizon

Unlike many investors who constantly buy and sell stocks, Buffett takes a patient and long-term approach to profitability. He believes in holding stocks for an extended period, allowing the power of compounding to work in his favor. Buffett's investment philosophy is encapsulated in his famous quote: "Our favorite holding period is forever."

3.3 Emphasis on Competitive Advantage and Moats

Buffett places great importance on identifying companies with sustainable competitive advantages, often referred to as having a "moat." He looks for businesses that possess unique qualities that make it difficult for competitors to replicate their success. This strategic focus on companies with durable competitive advantages further enhances the potential for long-term profitability.

4. Berkshire Hathaway: Warren Buffett's Business Holdings and Acquisitions

4.1 Overview of Berkshire Hathaway

Under Buffett's leadership, Berkshire Hathaway has evolved into a multinational conglomerate with diverse business interests. It owns a vast array of companies across industries, including insurance, energy, manufacturing, and retail. Berkshire Hathaway's stock is highly sought after by investors due to Buffett's reputation for delivering consistent returns over the years.

4.2 Diverse Portfolio of Investments

Aside from its wholly-owned subsidiaries, Berkshire Hathaway holds significant investments in various publicly-traded companies. These investments range from large-cap stocks to smaller businesses, reflecting Buffett's diverse approach to building wealth. The portfolio includes well-known names like Apple, Bank of America, and Coca-Cola, among others.

4.3 Key Acquisitions and Partnerships

Over the years, Berkshire Hathaway has made several notable acquisitions and partnerships. Some of the prominent acquisitions include the purchase of Burlington Northern Santa Fe, one of the largest railroads in North America, and Precision Castparts, a leading supplier of aerospace components. These strategic moves have allowed Berkshire Hathaway to expand its presence in different sectors and generate substantial returns for shareholders.

In summary, Warren Buffett's life, career, investment philosophy, and business empire are inspirational to aspiring investors and entrepreneurs. His remarkable success, combined with his down-to-earth nature and wit, have made him a beloved figure in the business world. Buffett's approach to investing and his commitment to long-term value creation continue to influence the current generations and generations to come.

5. Philanthropic Endeavors: Warren Buffett's Contributions to the World

5.1 The Giving Pledge and Philanthropic Philosophy

Warren Buffett's generosity extends far beyond his success in business and investment. Through his involvement in The Giving Pledge, a commitment by billionaires to donate the majority of their wealth to philanthropic causes, Buffett has left an indelible mark on the world of philanthropy. His philosophy centers around the idea that those who have been fortunate enough to amass great wealth should use their resources to help those in need. His leadership in promoting charitable giving has inspired countless individuals to follow suit and make a difference in their communities.

5.2 Donations and Impact on Education

Education is one area in which Warren Buffett's philanthropy has made a significant impact. He has donated billions to various educational initiatives, recognizing the importance of quality education in empowering individuals and improving communities. Through his contributions, Buffett has supported scholarships, funded educational programs, and championed efforts to improve access to education for underprivileged students. His dedication to education has opened doors and changed lives, emphasizing the transformative power of learning.

5.3 Initiatives in Global Health and Poverty Alleviation

In addition to his contributions to education, Warren Buffett has also made substantial contributions to global health and alleviation of poverty. His philanthropic endeavors have aimed to address pressing global challenges, such as eradicating diseases and improving healthcare access in underserved regions. Through partnerships with organizations like the Bill & Melinda Gates Foundation, Buffett has helped fund groundbreaking research, support vaccination campaigns, and promote innovative solutions to alleviate poverty and improve the well-being of people worldwide.

6. Lessons from Warren Buffett: Key Takeaways for Business and Investment

6.1 Importance of Patience and Long-Term Thinking

Warren Buffett's success in business and investment can be attributed, in part, to his emphasis on patience and long-term thinking. He famously advises investors to approach their decisions with a mindset focused on the long-term prospects of a company rather than on short-term market fluctuations. By staying focused on the underlying value of a business and ignoring short-term noise, Buffett has consistently made profitable investments and built wealth over time.

6.2 Focus on Fundamental Analysis and Intrinsic Value

Another key lesson from Warren Buffett is the importance of fundamental analysis and intrinsic value. Rather than getting caught up in market trends or speculative investments, Buffett advocates for a thorough evaluation of a company's financials, competitive advantages, and management quality. By understanding the intrinsic value of a business, investors can make informed decisions that align with their long-term goals and increase their chances of achieving sustainable returns.

6.3 Balancing Risk and Reward

While Warren Buffett is known for his conservative approach to investing, he also recognizes the importance of taking calculated risks. Buffett advises investors to seek opportunities that offer an attractive risk-reward ratio, emphasizing the need to understand the potential downsides while considering the potential rewards. By striking a balance between risk and reward, Buffett has achieved consistent returns while minimizing the potential for devastating losses.

7. Warren Buffett's Impact on the Business World: Influences and Legacy

7.1 Influence on Investors and Financial Markets

Warren Buffett's success and investment philosophy have had a profound impact on investors and the financial markets. His annual letters to shareholders and interviews are eagerly awaited by individuals seeking guidance and insights into the world of investing. Buffett's emphasis on value investing and long-term thinking has influenced countless investors, shaping their approach to wealth creation and investment strategy.

7.2 Buffett's Role as a Business Leader and Mentor

Beyond his contributions to investment, Warren Buffett's leadership and mentorship have helped shape the careers of many aspiring business leaders. His straightforward and down-to-earth advice, coupled with his willingness to share his wisdom, have earned him a reputation as a guiding figure in the business world. Many entrepreneurs and executives have looked to Buffett for guidance, recognizing his unparalleled success and his ability to navigate complex business landscapes.

7.3 Enduring Legacy and Cultural Impact

Warren Buffett's legacy endures and extends far beyond his financial achievements. His commitment to philanthropy and ethical business practices, and his engaging personality have made him a beloved figure in popular culture. The Oracle of Omaha has become synonymous with integrity, humility, and financial wisdom. His impact on the business world and society as a whole will continue to be felt for generations to come.

8. Conclusion: Warren Buffett's Enduring Influence and Legacy

Warren Buffett's remarkable journey from a young investor to one of the world's wealthiest individuals is a testament to his exceptional business acumen and philanthropic spirit. Through his philanthropic efforts, he has made a substantial impact on education, global health, and poverty alleviation. Meanwhile, his lessons on patience, fundamental analysis, and risk management continue to inspire and guide investors around the world. Buffett's influence as a business leader and mentor has shaped countless careers and his cultural impact is unparalleled. Warren Buffett's enduring legacy will serve as a beacon of inspiration for generations to come.

FAQs

1. What is Warren Buffett's investment philosophy?

Warren Buffett's investment philosophy revolves around value investing. He looks for companies with strong fundamentals, sustainable competitive advantages, and attractive valuations. Buffett focuses on long-term investments and holds stocks for extended periods, often avoiding short-term trading. His approach emphasizes thorough research, understanding a company's intrinsic value, and making decisions based on the underlying business rather than market fluctuations.

2. How did Warren Buffett build his business empire?

Warren Buffett built his business empire through astute investments and acquisitions. He started by acquiring Berkshire Hathaway, a textile manufacturing company, and transforming it into a diversified conglomerate. Over the years, Buffett strategically invested in various industries, including insurance, utilities, consumer goods, and technology. His ability to identify undervalued companies and capitalize on long-term opportunities played a significant role in expanding his empire and accumulating substantial wealth.

3. What philanthropic efforts has Warren Buffett undertaken?

Warren Buffett is known for his significant philanthropic efforts. He pledged the majority of his wealth to charitable causes through the Giving Pledge initiative. Buffett has focused his philanthropy mainly on educational initiatives, donating billions of dollars to improve educational systems and support scholarships. Additionally, he has directed substantial funds toward global health programs, poverty alleviation, and disaster relief efforts. Buffett's philanthropy aims to address societal challenges and create a positive impact on the world.

4. What is Warren Buffett's net worth?

His current net worth as at the time of this writing is estimated at $123.85 billion USD.

Warren Buffett's Golden Rule

- Rule No. 1 is never lose money.

- Rule No. 2 is never forget Rule No. 1.

Warren Buffett on value investing

- Price is what you pay. Value is what you get.

- Opportunities come infrequently. When it rains gold, put out the bucket, not the thimble.

- Widespread fear is your friend as an investor because it serves up bargain purchases.

- Whether we're talking about socks or stocks, I like buying quality merchandise when it is

marked down.

- We simply attempt to be fearful when others are greedy and to be greedy only when others are fearful. [Few quotes provide as much insight into the mind of Warren Buffet as this one.]

- The best thing that happens to us is when a great company gets into temporary trouble. We want to buy them when they're on the operating table.

[Be careful, however, about buying so-so businesses just because they're on sale]

- It's far better to buy a wonderful company at a fair price than a fair company at a wonderful price.

- For the investor, a too-high purchase price for the stock of an excellent company can undo the effects of a subsequent decade of favorable business developments.

- The key to investing is not assessing how much an industry is going to affect society, or

how much it will grow, but rather determining the competitive advantage of any given company and, above all, the durability of that advantage.

- On the margin of safety, which means, don't try and drive a 9,800-pound truck over a bridge that says it's, you know, capacity: 10,000 pounds. But go down the road a little bit and find one that says, capacity: 15,000 pounds.

Warren Buffett on investing for the long term

- You can't produce a baby in one month by getting nine women pregnant.

- Someone's sitting in the shade today because someone planted a tree a long time ago.

- If you aren't willing to own a stock for ten years, don't even think about owning it for ten minutes.

- When we own portions of outstanding businesses with outstanding managements, our favorite holding period is forever.

- An investor should act as though he had a lifetime decision card with just twenty punches on it.

- Since I know of no way to reliably predict market movements, I recommend that you purchase Berkshire shares only if you expect to hold them for at least five years. Those who seek short-term profits should look elsewhere.

- Buy a stock the way you would buy a house. Understand and like it such that you'd be content to own it in the absence of any market.

- All there is to investing is picking good stocks at good times and staying with them as long as they remain good companies.

- Do not take yearly results too seriously. Instead, focus on four or five-year averages.

- I never attempt to make money on the stock market. I buy on the assumption that they

could close the market the next day and not reopen it for five years.

- It is a terrible mistake for investors with long-term horizons -- among them pension funds, college endowments, and savings-minded individuals -- to measure their investment 'risk' by their portfolio's ratio of bonds to stocks.

Warren Buffett on dealing with losing investments

- Should you find yourself in a chronically leaking boat, energy devoted to changing vessels is likely to be a more productive than energy devoted to patching leaks.

Warren Buffett on the importance of a good reputation

- It takes 20 years to build a reputation and five minutes to ruin it. If you think about that, you'll do things differently.

- Lose money for the firm, and I will be understanding. Lose a shred of reputation for the firm, and I will be ruthless.

Warren Buffett on the right mindset for investing

- The most important quality for an investor is temperament, not intellect. You need a temperament that neither derives great pleasure from being with the crowd or against the crowd.

- The stock market is a no-called-strike game. You don't have to swing at everything -- you can wait for your pitch.

- Success in investing doesn't correlate with IQ ... what you need is the temperament to control the urges that get other people into trouble in investing.

- You don't need to be a rocket scientist. Investing is not a game where the guy with the 160 IQ beats the guy with 130 IQ.

Warren Buffett on avoiding fees and bad advice

- When trillions of dollars are managed by Wall Streeters charging high fees, it will usually be the managers who reap outsized profits, not the clients.

- Wall Street is the only place that people ride to in a Rolls Royce to get advice from those who take the subway.

- If returns are going to be 7 or 8 percent and you're paying 1 percent for fees, that makes an enormous difference in how much money you're going to have in retirement.

Warren Buffett on market crashes and recessions

- Only when the tide goes out do you discover who's been swimming naked.

- The years ahead will occasionally deliver major market declines -- even panics -- that will affect virtually all stocks. No one can tell you when these traumas will occur.

- Predicting rain doesn't count, building the ark does.

- This does not bother Charlie [Munger] and me. Indeed, we enjoy such price declines if we have funds available to increase our positions.

- The best chance to deploy capital is when things are going down.

- It's been an ideal period for investors: A climate of fear is their best friend. Those who invest only when commentators are upbeat end up paying a heavy price for meaningless reassurance.

Warren Buffett on the importance of cash

- "Too-big-to-fail" is not a fallback position at Berkshire. Instead, we will always arrange our affairs so that any requirements for cash we may conceivably have will be dwarfed by our own liquidity.

- We never want to count on the kindness of strangers in order to meet tomorrow's obligations. When forced to choose, I will not trade even a night's sleep for the chance of extra profits.

- Cash ... is to a business as oxygen is to an individual: never thought about when it is present, the only thing in mind when it is absent.

- The one thing I will tell you is the worst investment you can have is cash. Everybody is talking about cash being king and all that sort of thing. Cash is going to become worthless over time. But good businesses are going to become worth more over time.

Warren Buffett on stock-picking

- If you like spending six to eight hours per week working on investments, do it. If you don't, then dollar-cost average into index funds.

- Charlie and I view the marketable common stocks that Berkshire owns as interests in businesses, not as ticker symbols to be bought or sold based on their 'chart' patterns, the 'target' prices of analysts, or the opinions of media pundits.

- Buy into a company because you want to own it, not because you want the stock to go up."

- Never invest in a business you cannot understand.

- Risk comes from not knowing what you're doing. [A little bit of research can reduce a lot of risk. Buffett is ever the pedantic investment professor, and in this quote he reminds us that we should study, study, study.]

- If you don't feel comfortable making a rough estimate of the asset's future earnings, just forget it and move on.

- Buy companies with strong histories of profitability and with a dominant business franchise.

- We want products where people feel like kissing you instead of slapping you.

- It's better to have a partial interest in the Hope diamond than to own all of a rhinestone.

- In the business world, the rearview mirror is always clearer than the windshield.

- One thing that could help would be to write down the reason you are buying a stock before your purchase. Write down, "I am buying Microsoft at $300 billion because..." Force yourself to write this down. It clarifies your mind and discipline.

Warren Buffett on the importance of learning

- I just sit in my office and read all day.

- I insist on a lot of time being spent, almost every day, to just sit and think. That is very uncommon in American business.

- The most important investment you can make is in yourself.

- One can best prepare themselves for the economic future by investing in your own education. If you study hard and learn at a young age, you will be in the best circumstances to secure your future.

• Read 500 pages like this every day. That's how knowledge works. It builds up, like compound interest. All of you can do it, but I guarantee not many of you will do it.

Warren Buffett on ignoring market noise

• In the 54 years (Charlie Munger and I) have worked together, we have never forgone an attractive purchase because of the macro- or political environment, or the views of other people. In fact, these subjects never come up when we make decisions.

• In the 20th century, the United States endured two world wars and other traumatic and expensive military conflicts; the Depression; a dozen or so recessions and financial panics; oil shocks; a flu epidemic, and the resignation of a disgraced president. Yet the Dow rose from 66 to 11,497.

• We've long felt that the only value of stock forecasters is to make fortune tellers look good. Even now, Charlie and I continue to believe that short-term market forecasts are poison and should be kept locked up in a safe place, away from children and also from grown-ups who behave in the market like children.

• Most people get interested in stocks when everyone else is. The time to get interested is when no one else is. You can't buy what is popular and do well.

• Don't get caught up with what other people are doing. Being a contrarian isn't the key but being a crowd follower isn't either. You need to detach yourself emotionally.

- You are neither right nor wrong because the crowd disagrees with you. You are right because your data and reasoning are right.

Warren Buffett on America

- For 240 years it's been a terrible mistake to bet against America, and now is no time to start.

- American business -- and consequently a basket of stocks -- is virtually certain to be worth far more in the years ahead.

- I won't say if my candidate doesn't win, and probably half the time they haven't. I'm going to take my ball and go home.

Warren Buffett on knowing what not to invest in

- After 25 years of buying and supervising a great variety of businesses, Charlie and I have not learned how to solve difficult business problems. What we have learned is to avoid them.

- Speculation is most dangerous when it looks easiest.

- Investors should remember that excitement and expenses are their enemies.

- Keep things simple and don't swing for the fences. When promised quick profits, respond with a quick "no."

- What we learn from history is that people don't learn from history.

Warren Buffett on knowing your strengths and weaknesses

- There is nothing wrong with a 'know nothing' investor who realizes it. The problem is when you are a 'know nothing' investor but you think you know something.

- You only have to be able to evaluate companies within your circle of competence. The size of that circle is not very important; knowing its boundaries, however, is vital.

- We believe that a policy of portfolio concentration may well decrease risk if it raises, as it should, both the intensity with which an investor thinks about a business and the comfort-level he must feel with its economic characteristics before buying into it.

- Diversification is a protection against ignorance. It makes very little sense for those who know what they're doing.

Warren Buffett on avoiding spoiled kids

Believe it or not, Buffett is planning to give away 99% of his wealth to charity. His wife and kids will end up inheriting 1%, that amounts to a significant amount of money to support them and their posterity

- I believe in giving my kids enough so they can do anything, but not so much that they can do nothing.

Warren Buffett on debt

- If you buy things you do not need, soon you will have to sell things you need.

- You can't borrow money at 18 or 20 percent and come out ahead.

If you're smart, you're going to make a lot of money to make a lot of money without borrowing.

Warren Buffett on mortgages

- Because if you're wrong and rates go to 2 percent, which I don't think they will, you pay it off. It's a one-way renegotiation.

It is an incredibly attractive instrument for the homeowner, and you've got a one-way bet.

Warren Buffett on charitable giving

- If you're in the luckiest 1% of humanity, you owe it to the rest of humanity to think about the other 99%.

- We have learned to turn out lots of goods and services, but we haven't learned as well how to have everybody share in the bounty. The obligation of a society as prosperous as ours is to figure out how nobody gets left too far behind.

Warren Buffett on bitcoin

- Bitcoin has no unique value at all.

- You're just hoping the next guy pays more. And you only feel you'll find the next guy to pay more if he thinks he's going to find someone that's going to pay more. You aren't investing when you do that, you're speculating.

- Stay away from it. It's a mirage, basically...The idea that it has some huge intrinsic value is a joke in my view.

Warren Buffett on smart habits

- The difference between successful people and really successful people is that really successful people say no to almost everything.

- It's better to hang out with people better than you. Pick out associates whose behavior is better than yours and you'll drift in that direction.

Warren Buffett on great management

- When you have able managers of high character running businesses about which they are passionate, you can have a dozen or more reporting to you and still have time for an afternoon nap. Conversely, if you have even one person reporting to you who is deceitful, inept or uninterested, you will find yourself with more than you can handle.

- And so the important thing we do with managers, generally, is to find the .400 hitters and then not tell them how to swing.

Warren Buffett on stock buybacks

- When stock can be bought below a business's value it is probably the best use of cash.

- What is smart at one price is stupid at another.

[In other words, buybacks can be good or bad, depending on the price paid. If a company believes it is worth $100 per share and can buy stock for $90, it's a great use of capital. If the same company's stock is trading for $110, it's a bad move. Continuing on that point]:

- Many management [teams] are just deciding they're gonna buy X billions over X months. That's no way to buy things. You buy when selling for less than they are worth. ... It's not a complicated equation to figure out whether it is beneficial or not to repurchase shares.

Warren Buffett on gold

- I have no views as to where it (gold) will be, but the one thing I can tell you is it won't do anything between now and then except look at you. Whereas, you know, Coca-Cola will be making money, and I think Wells Fargo will be making a lot of money, and there will be a lot -- and it's a lot -- it's a lot better to have a goose that keeps laying eggs than goose that just sits there and eats insurance and storage and a few things like that.

- You could take all the gold that's ever been mined, and it would fill a cube 67 feet in each direction. For what it's worth at current gold prices, you could buy -- not some -- all of the farmland in the United States. Plus, you could buy 10 ExxonMobils, plus have $1 trillion of walking-around money. Or you could have a big cube of metal. Which would you take? Which is going to produce more value?

Warren Buffett on index funds

- Among the various propositions offered to you, if you invested in a very low-cost index fund -- where you don't put the money in at one time, but average in over 10 years -- you'll do better than 90% of people who start investing at the same time.

- Just pick a broad index like the S&P 500. Don't put your money in all at once; do it over a period of time

- It is not necessary to do extraordinary things to get extraordinary results.

In More of Warren Buffett's words:

Price is what you pay, value is what you get.

Never depend on a single income. Make an investment to create a second source.

Today people who hold cash equivalents feel comfortable. They shouldn't. They have opted for a terrible long-term asset, one that pays virtually nothing and is certain to depreciate in value.

Chapter 2

SUCCESS AND INNOVATION LESSONS FROM JEFF BEZOS

Jeff Bezos: The Man Behind Amazon's Success. An Introduction

Jeff Bezos, renowned entrepreneur and visionary, has played a pivotal role in transforming the landscape of e-commerce and reshaping the way we shop. As the founder and CEO of Amazon, Bezos has revolutionized the retail industry, turning a small online bookstore into a global powerhouse that offers an astonishing range of products and services. This article delves into Bezos' life and achievements, exploring his beginnings, the remarkable growth of Amazon, his innovative approaches, and the enduring impact he has had on business and technology.

1. Early Life and Entrepreneurial Beginnings

1.1 Childhood and Education

Jeff Bezos, the man behind Amazon's success, had humble beginnings. He was born on January 12, 1964, in Albuquerque, New Mexico. From an early age, Bezos showed signs of his future entrepreneurial spirit. As a child, he would dismantle his crib with a screwdriver just to see how it worked, much to his parents' amusement.

Bezos attended Miami Palmetto Senior High School, where he excelled academically. His love for computers and technology was evident even back then. After high school, he went on to study electrical engineering and computer science at Princeton University, where his analytical mind and problem-solving skills blossomed.

1.2 Early Influences and Ambitions

During his time at Princeton, Bezos was inspired by the rise of the internet and its potential for transforming various industries. He was particularly drawn to the idea of creating an online marketplace that could cater to a wide range of customers. This fascination with e-commerce and his determination to make his mark on the digital landscape laid the foundation for his future ventures.

Bezos' drive to take risks and pursue his ambitions was evident early on. After graduating from Princeton, he turned down lucrative job offers from established companies and instead decided to start his own business. Little did he know that this decision would lead him down a path towards building one of the most influential companies in the world.

2. The Birth of Amazon: From Online Bookstore to E-commerce Giant

2.1 Inception of Amazon

In 1994, Bezos founded Amazon as an online bookstore. The idea struck him during a cross-country road trip from New York to Seattle. He realized that the rapidly growing internet presented a unique opportunity to disrupt the traditional brick-and-mortar bookselling industry.

2.2 The First Steps: From Books to Everything

With humble beginnings in his garage, Bezos launched Amazon.com in July 1995. Initially, the focus was solely on selling books online, but Bezos had grander visions. He believed that the principles of customer-centricity, convenience, and limitless selection could apply to a wide range of products.

2.3 Scaling and Expansion of the Business

Amazon's exponential growth in its early years was driven by Bezos' relentless pursuit of customer satisfaction and his willingness to invest in new technologies. The company quickly expanded its offerings beyond books to include electronics, toys, and more. Bezos' bold decision to continuously reinvest profits into scaling the business allowed Amazon to become a dominant force in the e-commerce industry.

3. Innovations and Disruptions: How Bezos Transformed the Retail Industry

3.1 Introduction of Customer Reviews and Personalization

Bezos understood the power of customer reviews and ratings as a way to build trust and enhance the shopping experience. By allowing customers to share their opinions, Amazon revolutionized the way people made purchasing decisions online. This customer-centric approach fostered a sense of community and boosted sales.

3.2 Prime Membership Program: Revolutionizing Shipping and Streaming

One of Bezos' most significant innovations was the introduction of Amazon Prime in 2005. This membership program offered customers fast, free shipping on eligible items, and later expanded to include streaming services. Prime quickly became a game-changer for e-commerce, setting a new standard for convenience and customer loyalty.

3.3 Amazon Web Services (AWS): The Rise of Cloud Computing

In addition to its consumer-focused ventures, Bezos saw an opportunity to leverage Amazon's technological infrastructure to provide cloud computing services. Thus, Amazon Web Services (AWS) was born in 2006. AWS grew rapidly and became a leader in the cloud computing industry, offering scalable and cost-effective solutions to businesses of all sizes.

4. Amazon's Expanding Empire: Diversification and Acquisitions

4.1 Expansion into New Product Categories

Under Bezos' leadership, Amazon expanded its product offerings far beyond books, gradually becoming a one-stop-shop for everything from household essentials to fashion and electronics. This diversification allowed the company to cater to a broader customer base and solidify its position as a global e-commerce powerhouse.

4.2 Acquisitions and Strategic Partnerships

To further strengthen its market presence and fuel innovation, Bezos embarked on a series of strategic acquisitions and partnerships. Notable acquisitions include Zappos, Whole Foods Market, and Twitch, each of which brought expertise and market access to Amazon's expanding empire.

4.3 Building a Global Infrastructure

Bezos recognized the importance of building a robust logistical network to serve customers worldwide. Amazon invested heavily in warehouses, fulfillment centers, and transportation infrastructure, ensuring fast and reliable delivery across the globe. This commitment to infrastructure enabled Amazon to scale rapidly and solidify its position as the go-to online marketplace.

From his early days as a curious child to his transformation of Amazon into an e-commerce giant, Jeff Bezos' journey is a testament to his visionary leadership and relentless pursuit of customer satisfaction. His innovations and business strategies continue to shape the retail industry and inspire entrepreneurs around the world.

5. Bezos' Leadership Style: Vision, Risk-taking, and Long-term Thinking

5.1 Setting a Bold Vision for Amazon's Future

When it comes to setting a vision for the future, Jeff Bezos doesn't seem to settle for anything less than extraordinary. From the very beginning, Bezos had a grand vision for Amazon - to be the "Earth's most customer-centric company." This ambitious goal has shaped Amazon's growth and influenced its relentless pursuit of innovation. Bezos has always believed in thinking big and challenging the status quo, and his unwavering commitment to this vision has propelled Amazon to the top of the e-commerce industry.

5.2 Embracing Risk and Failure as a Path to Innovation

Bezos has never been one to shy away from taking risks. In fact, he embraces them. He understands that innovation requires experimentation and that failure is an inevitable part of the process. Bezos encourages his employees to take risks and learn from their failures, creating an environment where innovation can flourish. This willingness to take risks has led to groundbreaking products and services, such as the Kindle e-reader and Amazon Prime Video, which have revolutionized the way we read and shop online.

5.3 Fostering a Culture of Long-term Thinking

In a world obsessed with short-term gains, Bezos stands out as a long-term thinker. He believes that building a successful company requires patience and a commitment to long-term value creation. This philosophy is reflected in Amazon's approach to investing in future technologies and its relentless focus on customer satisfaction, even at the expense of short-term profits. Bezos's dedication to long-term thinking has not only helped Amazon weather the storms of the business world, but also has set an example for other companies to follow.

6. The Jeff Bezos Legacy: Philanthropy and Space Exploration

6.1 Bezos' Philanthropic Initiatives

Beyond his successes in business, Jeff Bezos also has made significant contributions to philanthropy. In 2018, he launched the Bezos Day One Fund, a $2 billion pledge to support programs addressing homelessness and quality education for underserved communities. Bezos has shown a commitment to making a positive impact on society and using his wealth to address critical issues.

6.2 Blue Origin: Bezos' Space Exploration Company

Not content with conquering Earth, Bezos has set his sights on the stars with his space exploration company, Blue Origin. Founded in 2000, Blue Origin aims to make space travel accessible and affordable for everyone. Bezos envisions a future where millions of people live and work in space, and Blue Origin is actively working towards this goal by developing reusable rockets and spacecraft. Bezos's passion for space exploration has ignited excitement and renewed interest in the possibilities beyond our planet.

7. Challenges and Controversies: Criticisms Faced by Bezos and Amazon

7.1 Labor Practices and Worker Conditions

While Amazon's success is undeniable, it has not been without its fair share of controversies. Of the main criticisms Bezos and

Amazon faced are their labor practices and worker conditions, including allegations of poor working conditions, long hours, and low wages in some of its fulfillment centers. Bezos has acknowledged these concerns and has committed to improving working conditions, but the issues remain a challenge for the company.

7.2 Antitrust Concerns and Market Dominance

As Amazon's dominance in the e-commerce market continues to grow, it has also attracted scrutiny from lawmakers and regulators. The company's market power has raised concerns about potential antitrust violations and unfair competition. Critics argue that Amazon's practices, such as using data from third-party sellers to develop its own competing products, give it an unfair advantage in the marketplace. Bezos and Amazon have been under pressure to address these concerns and ensure a level playing field for all participants in the market.

7.3 Privacy and Data Security Issues

With the rise of digital technology, concerns about privacy and data security have become increasingly important. Amazon, being a major player in the tech industry, has faced its fair share of scrutiny over these issues. From concerns about voice recordings collected by Amazon's virtual assistant, Alexa, to data breaches in its cloud services, the company has had to address these privacy and security concerns while maintaining customer trust.

8. The Enduring Impact: Bezos' Influence on Business and Technology

8.1 Revolutionizing E-commerce and Retail

Bezos' innovative approach to e-commerce has revolutionized the retail industry. Amazon's user-friendly interface, vast product selection, and efficient logistics have set new standards for online shopping. The company's success has forced traditional retailers to adapt and rethink their strategies to compete in the digital age.

8.2 Transforming the Way We Read with Kindle

With the introduction of the Kindle e-reader, Bezos transformed the way we read and consume books. The convenience of having thousands of books at your fingertips has made reading more accessible and enjoyable for countless people around the world. The Kindle's impact on the publishing industry cannot be overstated, as it has opened up new possibilities for authors and publishers.

8.3 Shaping the Future of Cloud Computing with Amazon Web Services

Amazon Web Services (AWS), Amazon's cloud computing division, has become a leader in the industry under Bezos' leadership. AWS provides scalable and reliable cloud computing services to businesses of all sizes, enabling them to focus on their core competencies without having to worry about infrastructure. AWS has not only transformed the way businesses operate, but also has fueled innovation by empowering startups and developers with the tools needed to bring their ideas to life.

8.4 Inspiring a New Generation of Entrepreneurs

Jeff Bezos' success story and entrepreneurial spirit have inspired countless aspiring entrepreneurs around the world. His journey from owning a small online bookstore to being the richest person on the planet serves as a reminder that anything is possible with a vision, persistence, and a willingness to take risks. Bezos' legacy goes beyond his own achievements; he has inspired a new generation of innovators and entrepreneurs to dream big and disrupt industries.

In conclusion, Jeff Bezos has undeniably left an indelible mark on the business world with his relentless pursuit of innovation, customer-centric approach, and long-term vision. From starting out as an online bookstore to becoming a diversified e-commerce giant, Amazon's success story is inextricably linked to Bezos' leadership and strategic decisions. Beyond Amazon, Bezos' philanthropic endeavors and dedication to space exploration through Blue Origin showcase his commitment to making a lasting impact on society and pushing the boundaries of human potential. Jeff Bezos' remarkable journey serves as an inspiration to aspiring entrepreneurs and a testament to the power of daring to think big and disrupt the status quo.

FAQs

1: How did Jeff Bezos come up with the idea for Amazon?

The idea for Amazon originated from Bezos' observation of the rapid growth of the internet and his belief that an online bookstore would be a compelling business opportunity. He recognized the potential to offer a vast selection of books that could be delivered directly to customers' doorsteps.

2: What are some of the key innovations introduced by Jeff Bezos at Amazon?

Bezos introduced several groundbreaking innovations at Amazon, such as customer reviews and personalized recommendations that enhanced the shopping experience. Additionally, the introduction of Amazon Prime, offering fast and free shipping along with exclusive access to streaming services, revolutionized customer loyalty programs.

3: What philanthropic initiatives has Jeff Bezos undertaken?

Jeff Bezos has undertaken significant philanthropic initiatives, including establishing the Bezos Day One Fund, focused on addressing homelessness and improving early childhood education.

Bezos has also pledged significant amounts to various environmental causes and has been actively involved in initiatives to combat climate change.

4: What is Blue Origin, and what is Jeff Bezos' involvement with it?

Blue Origin is a private aerospace company founded by Jeff Bezos with the goal of making space travel more accessible. Bezos is deeply involved with Blue Origin and has invested substantial resources into the company's research, development, and successful launches of reusable rockets.

4: What is Jeff Bezos' net worth?

Jeff Bezos' net worth as at the time of writing (2023) is estimated at $162.69 billion USD.

Jeff Bezos' Success Rules
Jeff Bezos on business:

- If you don't understand the details of your business you are going to fail.

- A brand for a company is like a reputation for a person. You earn reputation by trying to do hard things well.

- In business, what's dangerous is not to evolve.

- We've had three big ideas at Amazon that we've stuck with for 18 years, and they're the reason we're successful: Put the customer first. Invent. And be patient.

- If you're competitor-focused, you have to wait until there is a competitor doing something. Being customer-focused allows you to be more pioneering.

- You can have the best technology, you can have the best business model, but if the storytelling isn't amazing, it won't matter. Nobody will watch.

- Your margin is my opportunity.

- I knew that if I failed I wouldn't regret that, but I knew the one thing I might regret is not trying.

- I strongly believe that missionaries make better products. They care more. For a visionary, it's not just about the business. There has to be a business, and the business has to make sense, but that's not why you do it. You do it because you have something meaningful that motivates you.

- All businesses need to be young forever. If your customer base ages with you, you're Woolworth's.

- In the old world, you devoted 30% of your time to building a great service and 70% of your time shouting about it. In the new world, that inverts.

- There are two kinds of companies, those that work to try to charge more and those that work to charge less. We will be the second.

- We are stubborn on vision. We are flexible on details.

- If you only do things where you know the answer in advance, your company goes away.

- We've done price elasticity studies, and the answer is always that we should raise prices. We don't do that, because we believe -- and we have to take this as an article of faith -- that by keeping our prices very, very low, we earn trust with customers over time, and that that actually does maximize free cash flow over the long term.

- If you're long-term oriented, customer interests and shareholder interests are aligned.

- A company shouldn't get addicted to being shiny, because shiny doesn't last.

- All of my best decisions in business and in life have been made with heart, intuition, guts... not analysis.

- Sometimes we measure things and see that in the short term they actually hurt sales, and we do it anyway.

- We are comfortable planting seeds and waiting for them to grow into trees.

- There are two ways to extend a business. Take inventory of what you are good at and extend out from your skills. Or determine what your customers need and work backwards, even if it requires learning new skills.

- Friends congratulate me after a quarterly-earnings announcement and say, 'Good job, great quarter.' And I'll say, 'Thank you, but that quarter was baked three years ago.'

- What we need to do is always lean into the future; when the world changes around you and when it changes against you – what used to be a tailwind is now a headwind – you have to lean into that and figure out what to do because complaining isn't a strategy.

- If you do build a great experience, customers tell each other about that. Word of mouth is very powerful.

Jeff Bezos on innovation

- We innovate by starting with the customer and working backwards. That becomes the touchstone for how we invent.

- When [competitors are] in the shower in the morning, they're thinking about how they're going to get ahead of one of their top competitors. Here in the shower, we're thinking about how we are going to invent something on behalf of a customer.

- Market research doesn't help. If you had gone to a customer in 2013 and said, 'Would you like a black, always-on cylinder in your kitchen about the size of a Pringles can that you can talk to and ask questions, that also turns on your lights and plays music?' I guarantee you they'd have looked at you strangely and said, 'No, thank you.'

- I do get asked, quite frequently. 'What's gonna change in the next 10 years?' What I rarely get asked, and it's probably more important – and I encourage you to think about this – is the question, 'What's not going to change?' The answer to that question can allow you to organize your activities. You can work on those things with the confidence to know that all the energy you put into them today is still going to pay dividends in the years to come.

- Failure and invention are inseparable twins. To invent you have to experiment, and if you know in advance that it's going to work, it's not an experiment.

- I think frugality drives innovation, just like other constraints do. One of the only ways to get out of a tight box is to invent your way out.

- There'll always be serendipity involved in discovery.

- You have to be willing to be misunderstood if you're going to innovate.

- If you double the number of experiments you do per year, you're going to double your inventiveness.

- Invention requires a long-term willingness to be misunderstood. You do something that you genuinely believe in, that you have conviction about, but for a long period of time, well-meaning people may criticize that effort. When you receive criticism from well-meaning people, it pays to ask, 'Are they right?' And if they are, you need to adapt what they're doing. If they're not right, if you really have conviction that they're not right, you need to have that long-term willingness to be misunderstood. It's a key part of invention.

- One common pitfall for large organizations – one that hurts speed and inventiveness – is 'one-size-fits-all' decision making...The end result of this is slowness, unthoughtful risk aversion, failure to experiment sufficiently, and consequently diminished invention. We'll have to figure out how to fight that tendency.

- To get something new done you have to be stubborn and focused, to the point that others might find unreasonable.

- If you decide that you're going to do only the things you know are going to work, you're going to leave a lot of opportunity on the table.

- If you're watching your competitors, you're unlikely to invent a bunch of stuff on your own.

- Me-too' companies have not done that well over time.

Jeff Bezos on taking risks

- We take risks all the time, we talk about failure. We need big failures in order to move the needle. If we don't, we're not swinging enough. You really should be swinging hard, and you will fail, but that's okay.

- We all know that if you swing for the fences, you're going to strike out a lot, but you're also going to hit some home runs.

- The difference between baseball and business, however, is that baseball has a truncated outcome distribution. When you swing, no matter how well you connect with the ball, the most runs you can get is four. In business, every once in a while, when you step up to the plate, you can score 1,000 runs.

- If you're not stubborn, you'll give up on experiments too soon. And if you're not flexible, you'll pound your head against the wall and you won't see a different solution to a problem you're trying to solve.

- If you're not flexible, you'll pound your head against the wall and you won't see a different solution to a problem you're trying to solve.

- If you never want to be criticized, for goodness' sake don't do anything new.

- Companies are rarely criticized for the things that they failed to try. But they are, many times, criticized for things they tried and failed at.

- We understand that and believe in failing early and iterating until we get it right. When this process works, it means our failures are relatively small in size (most experiments can start small), and when we hit on something that is really working for customers, we double-down on it with hopes to turn it into an even bigger success.

- When you look at something, like, go back in time when we started working on Kindle almost seven years ago…. There you just have to place a bet. If you place enough of those bets, and if you place them early enough, none of them are ever betting the company. By the time you are betting the company, it means you haven't invented for too long.

Jeff Bezos on life and your career

- When you think about the things that you will regret when you're 80, they're almost always the things that you did not do. They're acts of omission. Very rarely are you going to regret something that you did that failed and didn't work or whatever.

- You can have a job, or you can have a career, or you can have a calling.

- If you can somehow figure out how to have a calling, you have hit the jackpot, cause that's the big deal.

- If you can make a decision with analysis, you should do so. But it turns out in life that your most important decisions are always made with instinct and intuition, taste, heart.

- Where you are going to spend your time and your energy is one of the most important decisions you get to make in life.

- The smartest people are constantly revising their understanding, reconsidering a problem they thought they'd already solved. They're open to new points of view, new information, new ideas, contradictions, and challenges to their own way of thinking.

- People who are right a lot listen a lot, and they change their mind a lot. People who are right a lot change their mind without a lot of new data. They wake up and reanalyze things and change their mind. If you don't change your mind frequently, you're going to be wrong a lot. People who are right a lot want to disconfirm their fundamental biases.

- Life's too short to hang out with people who aren't resourceful.

- In the end, we are our choices. Build yourself a great story.

- Cleverness is a gift; kindness is a choice. Gifts are easy – they're given after all. Choices can be hard.

- 'If I have three good decisions a day, that's enough,' he said. 'They should just be as high quality as I can make them.'

Jeff Bezos on customer service

- We see our customers as invited guests to a party, and we are the hosts. It's our job every day to make every important aspect of the customer experience a little bit better.

- The best customer service is if the customer doesn't need to call you, doesn't need to talk to you. It just works.

- The balance of power is shifting toward consumers and away from companies… The right way to respond to this if you are a company is to put the vast majority of your energy, attention and dollars into building a great product or service and put a smaller amount into shouting about it, marketing it.

- We don't focus on the optics of the next quarter; we focus on what is going to be good for customers.

- We invent before we have to. These investments are motivated by customer focus rather than by reaction to competition. We think this approach earns more trust with customers and drives rapid improvements in customer experience – importantly – even in those areas where we are already the leader.

- One advantage – perhaps a somewhat subtle one – of a customer-driven focus is that it aids a certain type of proactivity. When we're at our best, we don't wait for external pressures. We are internally driven to improve our services, adding benefits and features, before we have to. We lower prices and increase value for customers before we have to.

- Great innovations, large and small, are happening everyday [at Amazon] on behalf of customers.

Chapter 3

SUCCESS RULES FROM JACK MA, CHINA'S INNOVATIVE BILLIONAIRE

An Introduction to Jack Ma – His Life and Contributions

Jack Ma Yun, best known as Jack Ma, is a Chinese business magnate, investor and philanthropist. Born on September 10, 1964, he is the co-founder and former executive chairman of Alibaba Group, a multinational technology conglomerate. In addition, he co-founded Yunfeng Capital, a private equity firm. Ma is a strong proponent of an open and market-driven economy.

The life and achievements of Jack Ma Yun, the renowned Chinese entrepreneur, serve as a testament to the power of determination, innovation, and unwavering belief in one's dreams. From humble beginnings to becoming the co-founder of Alibaba Group, one of the world's largest e-commerce companies, Ma's journey has been nothing short of extraordinary. This article delves into the biography and life of Jack Ma, exploring his entrepreneurial journey, business strategies for success, contributions to e-commerce, valuable lessons from his leadership, philanthropic initiatives, and key milestones throughout his remarkable career.

1. Early Life and Education

1.1 Childhood and Family Background

Jack Ma Yun, the visionary entrepreneur behind Alibaba Group, was born on September 10, 1964, in Hangzhou, China. Growing up in a family of modest means, Ma experienced both the struggles and aspirations of an average Chinese household. His parents, traditional musicians by profession, instilled in him a strong work ethic and a sense of perseverance.

1.2 Education and Academic Journey

Despite his humble beginnings, Jack Ma's academic journey included some hurdles. He faced rejection multiple times during his school years, including failing his college entrance exam twice. His determination led him to eventually study English at Hangzhou Normal University, where he discovered his passion for learning and building connections with people from different cultures.

2. Entrepreneurial Journey: Founding Alibaba

2.1 From English Teacher to Internet Entrepreneur

After graduation, Ma faced another setback when job opportunities were limited for English teachers in China. Undeterred, he took a leap of faith and founded his own translation agency, which allowed him to explore the emerging field of the internet. This experience ignited his entrepreneurial spirit and set him on a path towards revolutionizing e-commerce.

2.2 The Birth and Growth of Alibaba

In 1999, Jack Ma, along with a group of friends, founded Alibaba, an online marketplace connecting Chinese manufacturers with global buyers. Initially, the company faced challenges and skepticism, but Ma's determination, strategic partnerships, and innovative solutions helped Alibaba become a leading platform in the e-commerce industry. The company's growth has been nothing short of remarkable, expanding its reach beyond trading goods to include various services and sectors.

3. Jack Ma's Business Strategies for Success

3.1 Embracing a Customer-Centric Approach

One of the key factors contributing to Alibaba's success is its unwavering focus on customers. Jack

Ma recognized the importance of providing exceptional user experiences and tailored services that helped Alibaba build a loyal customer base and maintain a competitive edge in the market.

3.2 Fostering Innovative Company Culture

Ma prioritized creating an environment that fostered innovation and risk-taking within Alibaba. He encouraged employees to think outside the box, embrace failure as a learning opportunity, and constantly push boundaries. This unique company culture has been instrumental in driving Alibaba's continuous growth and ability to adapt to changing market trends.

3.3 Expanding into Multiple Domains and Industries

With a visionary mindset, Jack Ma diversified Alibaba's business portfolio, venturing into sectors such as cloud computing, digital finance, and entertainment. This diversification strategy has allowed Alibaba to become a conglomerate, offering a wide range of services to its global customer base while further solidifying its position as a global e-commerce giant.

4. Contributions to E-commerce: Revolutionizing the Industry

4.1 Alibaba's Impact on the Chinese E-commerce Market

Jack Ma's Alibaba played a pivotal role in transforming the landscape of Chinese e-commerce. By providing small and medium-sized enterprises (SMEs) with a platform to reach global markets, Alibaba empowered these businesses and facilitated economic growth across China. The company's innovative logistics and financial solutions have also revolutionized the way goods are delivered and transactions are conducted online.

4.2 Introduction of Alibaba's Various Platforms

Alibaba's success extends beyond its e-commerce platform. The company has introduced various platforms and services, including Taobao (consumer-to-consumer marketplace), Tmall (business-to-consumer marketplace), and Alipay (digital payment platform). These platforms have further enriched the online shopping experience, making Alibaba a one-stop destination for consumers and businesses alike.

4.3 Global Expansion and International Influence

Under Jack Ma's leadership, Alibaba expanded its presence beyond China's borders, aiming to become a global powerhouse in e-commerce. The company's international acquisitions and investments in various countries have not only provided access to new markets but also facilitated cross-border trade and cultural exchange. Alibaba's influence continues to grow, shaping the future of global e-commerce.

In addition to his contributions to the business world, Jack Ma embraces philanthropy and actively advocates for environmental sustainability and education. Throughout his life, he has strived to inspire others with his entrepreneurship, resilience, and commitment to making a positive impact on society. Jack Ma Yun's journey serves as a testament to what can be achieved with passion, persistence, and a touch of whimsy.

5. Lessons from Jack Ma's Leadership and Vision

5.1 Inspiring Leadership Style and Management Principles

Jack Ma's leadership style is as unique as his personality. He believes in leading by example and inspiring his team through his own actions. Ma encourages his employees to think big, take risks, and pursue their passions. One of his famous quotes goes, "Today is hard, tomorrow will be worse, but the day after tomorrow will be sunshine."

His management principles emphasize the importance of teamwork, innovation, and customer satisfaction. He has always put customers first, believing that happy customers are the key to success. Ma also emphasizes the need for a positive work culture, where employees can have fun while delivering results.

5.2 Overcoming Challenges and Adapting to Change

Jack Ma's journey to success has been filled with challenges and obstacles. In the early years of Alibaba, he faced numerous rejections and failures, however, he never gave up and always found a way to turn setbacks into opportunities.

Ma believes in being adaptable and flexible in a constantly changing business landscape. He encourages his team to embrace change and view challenges as stepping stones to growth. His ability to pivot and innovate has allowed Alibaba to stay ahead of the curve and remain a dominant force in e-commerce.

5.3 Importance of Continuous Learning and Growth

Jack Ma is a strong advocate for continuous learning and personal growth. Despite not having a background in technology, he never shies away from learning new things. He believes that curiosity is the key to unlocking new opportunities.

Ma is a proponent of lifelong learning and encourages his employees to actively seek knowledge and acquire new skills. He believes that in a rapidly changing world, those who are willing to learn and adapt will be the ones who succeed.

6. Philanthropic Initiatives and Social Impact

6.1 The Establishment of Jack Ma Foundation

Driven by his belief in giving back, Jack Ma established the Jack Ma Foundation in 2014. The foundation's mission is to promote education, entrepreneurship, and environmental sustainability. Through the foundation, Ma aims to empower individuals and organizations to make a positive impact on society.

6.2 Philanthropic Projects and Initiatives

The Jack Ma Foundation has undertaken several philanthropic projects and initiatives. One notable initiative is the Rural Teacher Program, which aims to improve education in rural areas of China by providing training and support for teachers.

Another significant project is the Africa Netpreneur Prize Initiative, a program that aims to support and inspire African entrepreneurs. Through this initiative, Ma hopes to foster a spirit of entrepreneurship and unlock the potential of young African entrepreneurs.

6.3 Social Impact and Recognition

Jack Ma's philanthropic efforts have had a significant social impact. His initiatives have positively affected the lives of countless individuals, especially those in underserved communities. His dedication to education and entrepreneurship has helped create opportunities for people who previously had limited access to resources.

Ma's philanthropy has not gone unnoticed, and he has received recognition and accolades for his efforts. He was named one of the world's 100 most influential people by *Time* magazine and has received numerous awards for his contributions to society.

7. Key Milestones and Achievements in Jack Ma's Career

7.1 Honors, Awards, and Global Recognition

Throughout his career, Jack Ma has received numerous honors, awards, and global recognition for his achievements. He has been recognized as a visionary entrepreneur and a pioneer in the e-commerce industry.

Ma has been named Businessperson of the Year by *Fortune* magazine and received the Forbes Asia Businessman of the Year award. He was also included in Forbes' list of the world's most powerful people.

7.2 Notable Milestones and Achievements

Some notable milestones in Jack Ma's career include the founding of Alibaba Group in 1999, which has grown to become one of the world's largest e-commerce companies. In 2014, Alibaba had the largest initial public offering (IPO) in history, raising over $25 billion.

Ma's leadership has led to Alibaba's expansion into various sectors, including cloud computing, digital entertainment, and financial services. Under his guidance, Alibaba has become a global powerhouse, transforming the e-commerce landscape and pioneering new business models.

In conclusion, Jack Ma Yun's life and accomplishments stand as a beacon of inspiration for aspiring entrepreneurs and leaders around the globe. His relentless pursuit of innovation, unwavering determination, and commitment to making a positive impact have not only revolutionized the e-commerce industry but also reshaped the way we perceive success and philanthropy. Through his remarkable journey, Jack Ma has left an indelible mark on the business world, reminding us to dream big, embrace challenges, and always strive for excellence. As we reflect on his biography, life, business ventures, contributions to e-commerce, and philanthropy, we can draw invaluable lessons from his experiences and continue to be inspired by his enduring legacy.

FAQs

1. What were some of Jack Ma's key contributions to the e-commerce industry?

Jack Ma played a pivotal role in revolutionizing the e-commerce industry with the establishment of Alibaba Group. He introduced various platforms under Alibaba, such as Alibaba.com, Taobao, and Tmall, which transformed online shopping experiences. Additionally, Ma's vision and leadership propelled Alibaba's international expansion, making it a global powerhouse in the e-commerce domain.

2. How did Jack Ma's leadership style influence Alibaba's success?

Jack Ma's leadership style emphasizes embracing a customer-centric approach, fostering an innovative company culture, and promoting continuous learning and growth. He encourages his team to think outside the box, take risks, and adapt to changes in the industry. This enabled Alibaba to stay ahead of the curve and maintain its competitive edge.

3. What are some notable philanthropic initiatives undertaken by Jack Ma?

Jack Ma's philanthropic initiatives are primarily channeled through the Jack Ma Foundation. The foundation focuses on areas such as education, environmental protection, and entrepreneurship development. Notable projects include the Rural Teacher Program, which supports rural education in China, and the Africa Netpreneur Prize Initiative, which promotes entrepreneurship in Africa.

4. What can individuals learn from Jack Ma's journey and success?

From Jack Ma's journey, individuals can learn the importance of perseverance, embracing challenges, and adapting to change. His story emphasizes the significance of customer focus, innovation, and creating a positive impact on society. Jack Ma's success serves as a reminder that with passion, determination, and a strong vision, one can overcome obstacles and achieve remarkable success.

5. What is Jack Ma's net worth?

His net worth is estimated at $25.7 billion as at the time of writing (2023).

Rules for Success

- Get used to rejection.

- Keep your dream alive.

- Focus on culture.

- Ignore the # Littleman (someone who don't understand your idea).

- Get inspired.

- Stay focused.

- Have a good name (e.g Alibaba, Yahoo etc).

- Customer are # 1' Employees # 2; Shareholders # 3.

- Don't complain; look for opportunities and lastly..

- Have PASSION

Jack Ma quotes about business and job opportunities

- Never give up. Today is hard, tomorrow will be worse, but the day after tomorrow will be sunshine.

- Leadership is your instinct, then it's your training. Leaders are always positive, they never complain.

- Help young people. Help small guys. Because small guys will be big. Young people will have the seeds you bury in their minds, and when they grow up, they will change the world.

- A good boss is better than a good company.

- If you've never tried, how will you ever know if there's any chance?

- A leader should incentivize, but not with money. You give trust, respect, appreciation, and correct, heartfelt advice.

- Philanthropy is not about helping others; it's about helping yourself. When you change, the world changes.

- If you want to be successful, learn from other people's mistakes, not their successes. No matter how smart you are, you will encounter these mistakes, and you'll know how to deal with them.

- Once in your life, try something. Work hard at something. Try to change. Nothing bad can happen.

- If you don't give up, you still have a chance.

Jack Ma quotes that will inspire you to advance your career

- Today, making money is very simple. But making sustainable money while being responsible to the society and improving the world is very difficult.

- I always find people smarter than I am. Then my job is to make sure smart people can work together. Stupid people can work together easily, smart people can't.

- Life is so short, so beautiful. Don't be so serious about work. Enjoy life.

- Intelligent people need a fool to lead them. When the team's all a bunch of scientists, it is best to have a peasant lead the way. His way of thinking is different. It's easier to win if you have people seeing things from different perspectives.

- I don't want people to have deep pockets but shallow minds.

- As entrepreneurs, if you're not optimistic, you're in trouble. So the people I choose, they have to be optimistic.

- If there are nine rabbits on the ground, if you want to catch one, just focus on one.

- I'm not a tech guy. I'm looking at the technology with the eyes of my customers, normal people's eyes.

- Players should never fight. A real businessman or entrepreneur has no enemies. Once he understands this, the sky's the limit.

- I do everything to make sure my customer is happy, my employee is happy, society is healthy. I would focus on customers, I would focus on not making money, I would focus on making values.

Jack Ma quotes that will give you a unique perspective on wealth

- You've got to make your team have value, innovation, and vision.

- I call myself a blind man riding on a blind tiger.

- You should learn from your competitor but never copy. Copy and you die.

- Of course, you're not happy when people say 'no.' Have a good sleep, wake up, and try again.

- In my life, it's not how much we've achieved, it's how much we've gone through the tough days.

- When you are small, you have to be very focused and rely on your brain, not your strength.

- A leader should be visionary and have more foresight than an employee.

- Last century, people competed with muscle. This century, it's not muscle, it's wisdom. If a person wants to be successful he should have a high EQ. If he doesn't want to lose quickly, he should have a high IQ, but if he wants to be respected, he should have a high LQ, the Q of love.

- When people think too highly of you, you have the responsibility to calm down and be yourself.

- If machines can do things better, we have to change the way we teach. The key things are value, believing, independent thinking, teamwork, care for others, making sure humans are different from machines.

Jack Ma quotes

- My favorite movie is *Forrest Gump*. He said nobody makes money catching whales, people make money catching shrimps. So we serve small business.

- I don't want to be liked. I want to be respected.

- China is opening, opening the door. And internet is the best way to let the people understand what's happening outside.

- The next 30 years are going to be critical for the world. Make the technology inclusive, make the world change. Pay attention to those people who are 30 years old. Those are the internet generation. They will change the world.

- It doesn't matter if I failed. At least I passed the concept on to others. Even if I don't succeed, someone will succeed.

- Forget about your competitors, just focus on your customers.

- If we are a good team and know what we want to do, one of us can defeat ten of them.

- A leader should have higher grit and tenacity and be able to endure what the employees can't.

- The very important thing you should have is patience.

- I come to this world not to work, but to enjoy this life. I don't want to die in my office, I want to die on the beaches.

More Jack Ma quotes and sayings

- Before I'm 50 years old, my job is making money. After I'm 50 years old, my job is spending money, helping others, because you can't spend all that money.

- My job is to help more people have jobs.

- If you want to be successful tomorrow, it's impossible. If you want to be successful a year later, it's impossible. But if you want to win 10 years later, you have a chance.

- Try to find the right people, not the best people.

- If the customer loves you, the government will have to love you.

- We never lack money. We lack people with dreams, who can die for those dreams.

- If you don't do it, nothing's possible.

- Never, ever compete on prices, instead compete on services and innovation.

- Opportunity lies in the place where the complaints are.

- I always tell myself that we are born here not to work, but to enjoy life. We are here to make things better for one another.

Source: LinkedIn, https://www.linkedin.com/pulse/jack-mas-top-10-rules-successvery-inspiring-vishal-bora/ June 27, 2021. All rights reserved.

OPRAH WINFREY SUCCESS RULES

An Introduction to Oprah Winfrey: Her Life and Contributions

Oprah Winfrey is a name that has become synonymous with success, influence, and philanthropy. Born into humble beginnings, Oprah's journey to becoming one of the most powerful and influential women in the world is an awe-inspiring tale of determination, resilience, and unwavering ambition. From her groundbreaking talk show, *The Oprah Winfrey Show*, to her numerous business ventures and philanthropic contributions, Oprah's life serves as an inspiration for millions around the globe. In this article, we delve into the biography, life, business ventures, philanthropy, and the invaluable lessons we can learn from the remarkable journey of Oprah Winfrey.

1. Early Life and Background

1.1 Childhood and Family

Oprah Winfrey, a household name and one of the most influential figures in popular culture, was born on January 29, 1954, in Kosciusko, Mississippi. Growing up in poverty and facing numerous hardships, Oprah's childhood was far from glamorous. Raised by a single teenage mother and later by her grandmother, she faced many challenges that shaped her resilience and determination.

1.2 Challenges and Adversities

Oprah's early years were marked by adversity. She endured poverty, discrimination, and even abuse. Despite these harsh conditions, she managed to find solace and escape in reading and education. Her passion for learning became her ticket to a brighter future. As she overcame her difficult circumstances, Oprah developed an unwavering belief in the power of personal growth and self-improvement — an attitude that would later define her success.

2. Rise to Fame: The Oprah Winfrey Show

2.1 Early Career and Breakthrough

Oprah's journey to stardom began in the media industry, where she initially worked as a radio and television host. However, it was her role as the host of *The Oprah Winfrey Show* that catapulted her to the heights of fame. The show, which debuted in 1986, quickly gained a massive following due to Oprah's relatable style and ability to connect with her audience on a deeply personal level.

2.2 The Oprah Winfrey Show: Concept and Impact

What made *The Oprah Winfrey Show* stand out was its groundbreaking format. Oprah went beyond traditional talk shows by addressing topics that were often overlooked or considered taboo. From interviews with celebrities and world leaders to discussions on social issues, her show became a platform for open dialogue and personal growth. The impact of her program on popular culture cannot be overstated, as it paved the way for other influential talk shows and cemented Oprah's status as a media icon.

2.3 Memorable Moments and Guests

The Oprah Winfrey Show was filled with memorable moments that left a lasting impact on viewers. From Oprah's raw and emotional interviews with celebrities such as Tom Cruise and Michael Jackson to her legendary book club, there was never a shortage of captivating content. The show also featured groundbreaking segments on weight loss, self-help, and spirituality, earning Oprah a loyal fan base that admired her authenticity and genuine desire to make a difference.

3. Entrepreneurship and Business Ventures

3.1 Harpo Productions

Beyond television, Oprah's entrepreneurial spirit led her to establish Harpo Productions, a multimedia production company responsible for producing *The Oprah Winfrey Show*, as well as other successful television programs and films. Under her leadership, Harpo Productions became a powerhouse in the entertainment industry, showcasing Oprah's business acumen and knack for creating impactful content.

3.2 OWN Network

In 2011, Oprah ventured into cable television with the launch of the Oprah Winfrey Network (OWN). The network, co-owned by Oprah and Discovery, Inc., features a range of lifestyle programming, including talk shows, documentaries, and scripted series. Despite initial challenges, OWN has evolved into a platform that continues to showcase Oprah's commitment to empowering and inspiring audiences worldwide.

3.3 Book Club and Media Partnerships

Oprah's influence extends beyond television screens. Through her immensely popular book club, she has revolutionized the publishing industry and turned unknown authors into global sensations. Her media partnerships with major companies like Apple have allowed her to reach new audiences and support diverse storytelling. Oprah's ability to leverage her brand and platform for meaningful collaborations has solidified her status as a savvy businesswoman.

4. Philanthropic Endeavors and Contributions

4.1 The Oprah Winfrey Leadership Academy for Girls

Recognizing the importance of education, Oprah founded the Oprah Winfrey Leadership Academy for Girls in South Africa in 2007. The academy aims to provide quality education and leadership skills to girls from disadvantaged backgrounds. Oprah's personal investment in their success has had a transformative impact on the lives of these young women, empowering them to become leaders in their communities.

4.2 Oprah's Angel Network

Oprah's philanthropic efforts extend far and wide through her charitable foundation, Oprah's Angel Network. Over the years, she has supported various causes, including disaster relief, educational initiatives, and women's empowerment programs. Through her foundation, Oprah has made a tangible difference in the lives of countless individuals and communities, proving that generosity knows no bounds.

4.3 Support for Causes and Charities

In addition to her own initiatives, Oprah has used her platform and wealth to support numerous causes and charities. From advocating for child rights and equality to promoting wellness and environmental sustainability, she has demonstrated a deep commitment to making a positive impact on the world. Oprah's philanthropy serves as an inspiration for others to use their influence and resources to create meaningful change.

5. Lessons from Oprah's Journey

5.1 Overcoming Obstacles and Resilience

Oprah Winfrey's journey is a testament to the power of resilience and the ability to overcome obstacles. From a challenging childhood marked by poverty and abuse, Oprah faced numerous adversities on her path to success, however, she never let these hardships define her or dampen her spirit. Instead, she harnessed her experiences as fuel for personal growth and resilience.

One of the key lessons we can learn from Oprah is the importance of resilience in the face of adversity. Life may throw unexpected challenges our way, but it's how we respond to them that truly matters. Oprah's ability to bounce back from misfortune, and never losing sight of her dreams, are an inspiration to us all.

5.2 Embracing Authenticity and Empathy

Authenticity and empathy are two qualities that have played a significant role in Oprah's success. Throughout her career, she has dedicated herself to connecting with people on a genuine level, sharing her own experiences, and empathizing with their struggles. This authentic approach has resonated with millions around the world and helped her build a strong and loyal fan base.

In a world that often encourages conformity, Oprah teaches us the power of embracing our true selves. By being authentic, we not only gain a sense of fulfillment but also attract genuine connections and opportunities. Additionally, Oprah's empathy reminds us of the importance of showing compassion toward others and using our platform to uplift and empower those around us.

5.3 Pursuing Passion and Purpose

Passion and purpose are at the core of Oprah's extraordinary success. From her early days as a talk show host to her media empire and philanthropic endeavors, Oprah's unwavering dedication to pursuing her passions has been the driving force behind her achievements.

Oprah teaches us that when we align our actions with our passions and values, success becomes more than just a goal — it becomes a natural outcome. By following our passions and living with purpose, we can unlock our full potential and create a meaningful impact in our own lives and the lives of others.

For many individuals, Oprah Winfrey's journey is not just a biography of a remarkable individual, but a blueprint for personal and professional growth. Her story teaches us the importance of resilience in the face of obstacles, embracing our authenticity and empathy, and pursuing our passions and purpose. By embodying these lessons, we can inspire others and create a positive impact in our own lives and the world around us.

In summary, Oprah Winfrey's biography is a testament to the power of resilience, determination, and the pursuit of one's passions. From humble beginnings, she rose to become a global influencer, media mogul, and philanthropist. Through her relatable style, entrepreneurial ventures, and philanthropic endeavors, she has left an indelible mark on the world, inspiring others to dream big, embrace authenticity, and make a difference.

FAQs

1. What were some of Oprah Winfrey's major business ventures?

Oprah Winfrey has been involved in various successful business ventures throughout her career. Some of the major ones include Harpo Productions, which produced her highly popular talk show, *The Oprah Winfrey Show*, and later expanded into film and television production. She also launched the Oprah Winfrey Network (OWN), a cable and satellite television channel, and established the influential Oprah's Book Club.

2. How has Oprah Winfrey contributed to philanthropy?

Oprah Winfrey has been a dedicated philanthropist, using her wealth and influence to make a significant impact on various causes. She founded the Oprah Winfrey Leadership Academy for Girls in South Africa, providing education and opportunities to underprivileged girls. She also established Oprah's Angel Network, which supported numerous charitable initiatives. Additionally, Oprah has been a vocal advocate for causes like education, women's rights, and poverty alleviation.

3. What are some key lessons we can learn from Oprah's journey?

Oprah Winfrey's life and achievements offer valuable lessons for individuals aspiring to success and personal growth. Some key lessons include the importance of perseverance in the face of adversity, embracing authenticity and staying true to oneself, and displaying empathy and compassion towards others. Oprah also emphasizes the significance of pursuing passions and purpose, as well as leveraging one's platform to uplift and empower others.

4. What is Oprah Winfrey's net worth?

Oprah Winfrey's current net worth at time of writing (2023) is estimated at $2.81 billion USD.

Success Rules of Oprah Winfrey

1. Rather than overwhelming yourself with the big picture, ask yourself what the next right move is.

It's easy to feel intimidated by everything on your plate, so instead of facing such an enormous proposition, take things one step at a time. Make the best next move you can, then make the next move, and then the next one, each time going as carefully and as thoughtfully as you can. Winfrey believes that success isn't one giant leap — it's a series of baby steps. And, if you make one misstep, understand that your life and your career won't be defined by that one mistake. You have more steps to take, and you'll arrive at success eventually.

2. When you see an opportunity, take it.

Oprah does not chalk up any of her success to luck. Instead, she insists there's been grace and blessings, but there's also been opportunity. The key to being successful is to recognize when opportunity is in front of you and seize it. So what about luck? Winfrey has said, "Luck is preparation meeting the moment of opportunity." If you're not prepared, if you're not looking for that chance, then luck won't do you any good.

3. Forgive yourself for your past mistakes.

You're not the person you were five, ten, twenty, or more years ago. A lot of wisdom just comes with age, so don't beat yourself up for youthful transgressions. You didn't know any better — but you know better now! Look at those past mistakes as teachable opportunities, learn as much as you can from them, and then move forward.

4. Never stop improving yourself.

This means continually working on your personality, your skill set, and your network so that you are in the best possible position to make a difference. Others may see your efforts to improve yourself as self-centeredness, or being "full of yourself," but Winfrey believes you should ignore them. You always need to be improving if you want to get ahead. If people are saying that about you, take it as a compliment. You're doing a lot, and others are noticing.

5. Go as hard as you can.

Beyond that, recognize that you have control only over your own performance. You can't control the competition at all. When Winfrey was starting out with her talk show, she knew that there were lots of other shows competing for guests, topics, and airtime, but she also knew that she had no control over any of that. All she could do was make the best show she knew how to make. Similarly, all you can do is the best you know how, all the time. It's like a race: you just run hard until you reach the finish line. All you can do is make yourself run more quickly, not make your competition run more slowly. That's what brings you success: building yourself up, not looking behind you to see where your competition is.

6. Don't just dream — believe.

It's OK to have big dreams for yourself; we all do. But if you're going to be successful, you've got to do more than dream. You have to believe that the life you aspire to lead will one day be yours. Winfrey always knew that she would live a big, fulfilling life; she had that strong belief in what her future held. Do the same, and hold firmly to that belief, even in the most difficult times, and you're likely to get exactly where you want to be.

7. Remember that people are more alike than they are different.

We're all seeking the same thing. Winfrey will tell you we all want to reach our fullest potential. Sure, we all go about that in different ways, because we all have different skills and different passions, but at the end of the day, we all just want to be true to ourselves and be, as Winfrey might say, the "truest expression" of ourselves.

8. Find your purpose in life.

If you're going to be successful, according to Winfrey, you need to figure out why you're here on Earth. Most entrepreneurs already feel like they know their purpose, but if you don't, stop! Put everything on pause, take some time for genuine soul searching and self-reflection, and find your purpose.

9. Keep yourself grounded and centered.

It's easy to get lost in your work, and it's easy to let your ego inflate, but if you keep your focus, stay compassionate, and always seek to understand and connect with others; you'll improve your chances of success substantially. Winfrey attributes much of her own personal success to her ability to keep herself grounded.

10. Try to remember that everything will be OK.

If you're aiming for big time success, you've got to take the long view. Yes, it's natural to be a little scared, but never lose faith that everything will work out just fine.

11. Fear – Channel It

The thing you fear most has no power. Your fear of it is what has the power. Facing the truth really will set you free."

12. Failure – Refuse It

I don't believe in failure. It is not failure if you enjoyed the process.

13. Success – Envision It

I had no idea that being your authentic self could make me as rich as I've become. If I had, I'd have done it a lot earlier.

14. Work - Fun

You know you are on the road to success if you would do your job, and not be paid for it.

When you're doing the work you're meant to do, it feels right and every day is a bonus, regardless of what you're getting paid.

What I know is, is that if you do work that you love, and the work fulfills you, the rest will come.

15. Passion Plays

Passion is energy. Feel the power that comes from focusing on what excites you. Forget about the fast lane. If you really want to fly, harness your power to your passion. Honor your calling. Everybody has one. Trust your heart, and success will come to you.

16. Significance Matters Most

The key to realizing a dream is to focus not on success but significance - and then even the small steps and little victories along your path will take on greater meaning. The more you praise and celebrate your life, the more there is in life to celebrate.

How do I define success? Let me tell you, money's pretty nice. But having a lot of money does not automatically make you a successful person. What you want is money and meaning. You want your work to be meaningful because meaning is what brings the real richness to your life.

17. Change is a Choice

I believe the choice to be excellent begins with aligning your thoughts and words with the intention to require more from yourself.

Doing the best at this moment puts you in the best place for the next moment.

The greatest discovery of all time is that a person can change his future by merely changing his attitude.

18. Humility – Exude It

Be thankful for what you have; you'll end up having more. If you concentrate on what you don't have, you will never, ever have enough.

Oprah Winfrey Quotes about Success, Self-Esteem, and Self-Love

- Turn your wounds into wisdom.

Turn your mess into a message. Don't let your pain be in vain. Do something positive with it!

- You can have it all. Just not all at once.

  Be patient. Have an order. Prioritize. Focus on what you want, now. Plan for what you want later.

- If a man wants you, nothing can keep him away. If he doesn't want you, nothing can make him stay.

  All you can do is be yourself, that is the only thing you can control. Focus on that.

- I've come to believe that each of us has a personal calling that's as unique as a fingerprint – and that the best way to succeed is to discover what you love and then find a way to offer it to others in the form of service, working hard, and also allowing the energy of the universe to lead you.

- Embrace your uniqueness. You are different, your gift is special – own it and unapologetically share it with the world.

- Real integrity is doing the right thing, knowing that nobody's going to know whether you did it or not. You know you reached a high level of integrity when you don't even care if people know or not. You just do it.

- The more you praise and celebrate your life, the more there is in life to celebrate. Never become too busy or too preoccupied to celebrate everything you have done, all that you have, and all that you are!

- One of the hardest things in life to learn is which bridges to cross and which bridges to burn. You can't keep all of them. You can't make everyone happy.

- You don't become what you want, you become what you believe. There is nothing more influential than your thoughts.

- When you undervalue what you do, the world will undervalue who you are. Love yourself and all the world will love you too!

- Self-esteem comes from being able to define the world in your own terms and refusing to abide by the judgments of others. A true sign of confidence is when you are able to break away from the crowd, regardless of what others say or think.

- Only make decisions that support your self-image, self-esteem, and self-worth. Become extremely intentional with everything that you do. Be fully on purpose. Make sure everything you do supports who you are and who you want to be.

- It makes no difference how many peaks you reach if there was no pleasure in the climb. Enjoy your journey. So when people ask you, 'How did you do it?' you have a great story to tell.

- Forgiveness is giving up the hope that the past could have been any different. Stress comes from thinking that things should have been different. But they have worked out this way for a reason. ALL you can do is keep moving forward.

- You are where you are in life because of what you believe is possible for yourself.

Oprah Winfrey quotes about failure

- So go ahead. Fall down. The world looks different from the ground. Everything that we go through gives us a new perspective, information, and insight. Embrace all of it.

- I don't believe in failure. It's not failure if you enjoy the process. There is no failure, only feedback. Everything is either what you want, or what you don't want. But failure is not real.

- When people show you who they are ... believe them! Trust your intuition. People are more transparent than you might think.

More Oprah Winfrey quotes about life and success

- Dogs are my favorite role models. I want to work like a dog, doing what I was born to do with joy and purpose. I want to play like a dog, with total, jolly abandon. I want to love like a dog, with unabashed devotion and complete lack of concern about what people do for a living, how much money they have, or how much they weigh. The fact that we still live with dogs, even when we don't have to herd or hunt our dinner, gives me hope for humans and canines alike.

- Your calling isn't something that somebody can tell you about. It's what you feel. It is the thing that gives you juice. The thing that you are supposed to do. And nobody can tell you what that is. You know it inside yourself.

More quotes by Oprah about love and life

- It all boils down to one thing...it is your 'relationship' to the source, and that relationship to that which we call God, or don't call God, or don't even know...is God.

- It is ALL that really matters...when you surrender, and stop resisting, and stop trying to change that which you cannot change, but be in the moment, be fully open to the blessings you have already received, and those that are yet to come to you, and stand in that space of gratitude, and honor, and claim that for yourself, and look at where you are, and how far you have come, and what you've gotten, and what you've accomplished, and who you are.

- When you can claim 'that', and see that, the literal vibration of your life will change. The vibration of your life will change."

- I was once afraid of people saying, 'Who does she think she is?' Now I have the courage to stand and say, 'This is who I am.'

- Books were my pass to personal freedom. I learned to read at age three, and discovered there was a whole world to conquer what went beyond our farm in Mississippi.

- You've got to follow your passion. You've got to figure out what it is you love—who you really are. And have the courage to do that. I believe that the only courage anybody ever needs is the courage to follow your own dreams.

- Beginning when we are girls, most of us are taught to deflect praise. We apologize for our accomplishments. We try to level the field with our family and friends by downplaying our brilliance. We settle for the passenger's seat when we long to drive. That's why so many of us have been willing to hide our light as adults. Instead of being filled with all the passion and purpose that enable us to offer our best to the world, we empty ourselves in an effort to silence our critics. The truth is that the naysayers in your life can never be fully satisfied. Whether you hide or shine, they'll always feel threatened because they don't believe they are enough. So stop paying attention to them. Every time you suppress some part of yourself or allow others to play you small, you are ignoring the owner's manual your Creator gave you. What I know for sure is this: You are built not to shrink down to less but to blossom into more. To be more splendid. To be more extraordinary. To use every moment to fill yourself up.

- I would like to thank the people who've brought me those dark moments, when I felt most wounded, betrayed. You have been my greatest teachers.

- Wherever you are in your journey, I hope you, too, will keep encountering challenges. It is a blessing to be able to survive them, to be able to keep putting one foot in front of the other — to be in a position to make the climb up life's mountain, knowing that the summit still lies ahead. And every experience is a valuable teacher.

- Forgiveness is letting go of the hope that the past can be changed.

- When you make loving others the story of your life, there's never a final chapter, because the legacy continues. You lend your light to one person, and he or she shines it on another and another and another. And I know for sure that in the final analysis of our lives- when the to-do lists are no more, when the frenzy is finished, when our e-mail inboxes are empty- the only thing that will have any lasting value is whether we've loved others and whether they've loved us.

- When the talk about my troubles was loudest, I did the thing I've always spoken of most. I got still and listened for the answer to What is this here to teach me? The answer, first and foremost? Lay your ego down. Step out of your ego so you can recognize the truth. As soon as I did that, I was able to see the role I had played in creating "my circumstances," without blaming other people. And — bingo! — I realized that all the noise about my struggle was a reflection of my personal angst and fear.

Oprah Winfrey quotes to empower

- With every experience, you alone are painting your own canvas, thought by thought, choice by choice.

- It doesn't matter who you are, where you come from. The ability to triumph begins with you – always.

- Breathe. Let go. And remind yourself that this very moment is the only one you know you have for sure.

- My idea of heaven is a great big baked potato and someone to share it with.

- I have a lot of things to prove to myself. One is that I can live my life fearlessly.

- Even people who believe they deserve to be happy and have nice things often don't feel worthy once they have them.

- I don't want anyone who doesn't want me.

- Think like a queen. A queen is not afraid to fail. Failure is another stepping stone to greatness.

- Create the highest, grandest vision possible for your life, because you become what you believe.

- You know you are on the road to success if you would do your job and not be paid for it.

Sources: Every day power, https://everydaypower.com/oprah-winfrey-quotes-about-life/. June 28, 2021. All rights reserved.

Money INC, https://moneyinc.com/10-rules-success-according-oprah-winfrey/ June 28, 2021. All rights reserved

Forbes, https://www.forbes.com/sites/johngreathouse/2012/09/27/23-leadership-tips-from-oprah-winfrey/?sh=54eba5801a5d June 28, 2021. All rights reserved.

Chapter 5

ELON MUSK'S SUCCESS RULES

Elon Musk: His Life and Contributions

Elon Musk, a name synonymous with innovation and ambition, has made an indelible mark on the world through his remarkable achievements and groundbreaking ventures. Musk's journey from an imaginative child to a visionary entrepreneur has captivated the imagination of millions. This article delves into the fascinating life and incredible accomplishments of Elon Musk, exploring his early years; entrepreneurial endeavors, contributions to sustainable technology and clean energy, revolutionary advancements in the space industry, philanthropic initiatives, as well as the controversies and challenges he has faced. Furthermore, we will examine Musk's compelling vision for the future and the enduring legacy he is shaping for generations to come.

1. Early Life and Education

1.1 Childhood and Family Background

Before Elon Musk became a household name, he was just a regular kid with big dreams and even bigger imaginations. Born in Pretoria, South Africa, on June 28, 1971, Musk had a childhood filled with curiosity and a thirst for knowledge. His parents, Maye and Errol Musk, played a significant role in shaping his love for science and technology. Maye was a Canadian model and dietician, while Errol was an engineer and pilot. With such a combination of genes, it's no wonder Musk turned out to be the ultimate high-flying entrepreneur!

1.2 Education and Academic Pursuits

Like many successful people, Musk's educational journey had its fair share of twists and turns. He attended Waterkloof House Preparatory School and later moved to the prestigious Pretoria Boys High School. Musk's passion for reading and learning led him to devour encyclopedias and delve deep into subjects like physics, computer programming, and engineering.

At the age of 17, Musk left South Africa to escape mandatory military service and pursue higher education. He enrolled at Queen's University in Canada and transferred to the University of Pennsylvania, where he earned degrees in physics and economics. Armed with a strong foundation in science and a keen business sense, Musk was ready to take on the world and leave his mark on the entrepreneurial landscape.

2. Entrepreneurial Ventures and Business Successes

2.1 Zip2 Corporation: The Early Startup

Musk's entrepreneurial journey began with the creation of Zip2 Corporation in 1995. This software company aimed to assist newspapers in establishing an online presence, something that was still a novelty at the time. Despite facing many hurdles and having to sleep in the office to save money, Musk's determination paid off when Compaq acquired Zip2 for an impressive $307 million in 1999. It was a taste of success that would only serve to fuel Musk's ambitions further.

2.2 X.com and the Birth of PayPal

After the Zip2 success, Musk didn't sit back and relax. Instead, he dove headfirst into the world of online payments and founded

X.com, an online payment company. Eventually, X.com transformed into PayPal, revolutionizing how people send and receive money online. In 2002, eBay acquired PayPal for a staggering $1.5 billion, solidifying Musk's place as one of the leading innovators in the business world.

2.3 Tesla Motors: Revolutionizing the Electric Car Industry

Musk's audacious ambitions didn't stop at internet payment systems. In 2004, he co-founded Tesla Motors, a company that aimed to accelerate the world's transition to sustainable transportation. Despite facing skepticism and challenges, Musk pushed Tesla to become a trailblazer in the electric car industry. With sleek designs, impressive performance, and a focus on renewable energy, Tesla has become synonymous with cutting-edge and eco-friendly transportation.

2.4 SpaceX: Pioneering Private Space Exploration

No stranger to lofty goals, Musk set his sights on the final frontier: Space. In 2002, he founded SpaceX, with the mission to make space exploration more accessible and affordable. Musk's vision for humanity's future among the stars propelled SpaceX to achieve remarkable milestones, including reusable rockets and successful cargo resupply missions to the International Space Station. SpaceX has boldly redefined the possibilities of private space travel.

2.5 Other Notable Ventures and Business Interests

Elon Musk's entrepreneurial spirit knows no bounds. In addition to Tesla and SpaceX, he has been involved in various other ventures. October 27, 2022, he acquired Twitter Inc., which he renamed X in 2023. Musk co-founded Neuralink, a company focused on developing implantable brain-machine interfaces. He is also the driving force behind The Boring Company, which aims to revolutionize tunneling technology for efficient transportation systems. And let's not forget his fascination with flame throwers, as evidenced by his eccentric venture, The Boring Company's Not a Flamethrower. Musk's business interests span an incredible range of industries, demonstrating his insatiable appetite for innovation and disruption.

3. Contributions to Sustainable Technology and Clean Energy

3.1 The Vision for a Sustainable Future

Elon Musk is not just an entrepreneur; he is also a passionate advocate for sustainability and clean energy. He envisions a future where renewable energy sources replace fossil fuels and where humanity's impact on the environment is minimized. This commitment to a better world influences all of Musk's endeavors, from electric cars to solar energy solutions.

3.2 SolarCity: Advancing Solar Energy Solutions

Recognizing the immense potential of solar energy, Musk co-founded SolarCity in 2006. The company aimed to make solar power more accessible and affordable for residential and commercial use. SolarCity's innovative leasing model, which eliminated the upfront costs of installing solar panels, proved a game-changer for the industry. Today, SolarCity, now a part of Tesla, continues to make strides in advancing solar energy technology and empowering individuals to embrace clean energy solutions.

3.3 Powerwall and Powerpack: Revolutionizing Energy Storage

Musk understands that renewable energy sources like solar and wind can be intermittent, which is where effective energy storage becomes crucial. Enter the Powerwall and Powerpack, two groundbreaking inventions from Tesla. These energy storage solutions allow homes, businesses, and even entire regions to store excess renewable energy for use during periods of high demand or low production. With the Powerwall and Powerpack, Musk is helping pave the way for a future where clean energy can be reliably harnessed and utilized on demand.

4. Revolutionizing the Space Industry

4.1 Founding SpaceX and Overcoming Challenges

SpaceX, founded by Elon Musk in 2002, has become a force to be reckoned with in the space industry. However, the road to success was not without its hurdles. In the early days, SpaceX faced multiple rocket failures and financial difficulties. Nevertheless, Musk's perseverance and belief in the company's mission led SpaceX to overcome challenges that would have deterred others. Failure became a stepping stone on the path to revolutionizing space exploration.

4.2 Achievements and Milestones in Space Exploration

Under Musk's leadership, SpaceX achieved several significant milestones that were once thought impossible for a private company. In 2012, SpaceX became the first commercial company to send a spacecraft, the Dragon, to the International Space Station and return it safely to Earth. This accomplishment marked a turning point in space exploration, highlighting the potential for private companies to contribute to humanity's quest for knowledge beyond our planet.

4.3 The Starship Program and the Plan for Mars Colonization

Musk's ultimate vision for SpaceX is nothing short of awe-inspiring: Colonizing Mars. Through the ambitious Starship program, SpaceX aims to develop a fully reusable spacecraft capable of carrying humans and cargo to other planets. Musk dreams of establishing a self-sustaining colony on Mars. He believes that becoming a multi-planetary species is vital for the long-term survival of humanity. Through SpaceX, he is developing the technology and infrastructure required to enable humans to colonize Mars and other celestial bodies.

Musk's ambitious plan involves the development of the Starship, a fully reusable spacecraft designed to transport humans and cargo to Mars. He envisions a future where humans can establish self-sustaining settlements on the Red Planet, ultimately making humanity an interplanetary species.

By pushing the boundaries of space exploration and technology, Musk aims to inspire future generations to look beyond Earth's constraints and explore the vast possibilities the universe has to offer.

5. Philanthropy and Social Impact Initiatives

5.1 Musk Foundation: Supporting Education, Renewable Energy, and Humanitarian Causes

When Elon Musk isn't busy launching rockets into space or revolutionizing the electric vehicle industry, he's also dedicated to making a positive impact on the world through his philanthropic endeavors. Through his Musk Foundation, he has donated millions of dollars to various causes, with a focus on education, renewable energy, and humanitarian efforts.

Musk has a strong belief in the power of education and has donated significant funds towards educational initiatives. The Musk Foundation has supported organizations like the Khan Academy, which provides free, quality education to anyone with an internet connection. Musk's contribution helps ensure that education is accessible to people from all walks of life, regardless of their socioeconomic background.

In addition to education, Musk has also directed his efforts towards promoting and advancing renewable energy. He has made substantial donations to projects focused on solar energy research and development, aiming to accelerate the transition to a sustainable future. By investing in renewable energy, Musk envisions a world free from dependence on fossil fuels and the harmful emissions they produce.

Musk's philanthropy extends beyond education and renewable energy. He has also supported humanitarian causes, including disaster relief efforts. One notable example is his pledge to help rebuild areas affected by natural disasters, such as providing assistance after the devastating wildfires in California.

5.2 OpenAI and Neuralink: Advancing AI and Brain-Computer Interface Research

Elon Musk is not just interested in making impactful contributions on Earth; he is also keen on exploring and advancing the frontiers of technology. This can be seen through his involvement in ventures like OpenAI and Neuralink. Through initiatives like OpenAI and Neuralink, Musk is pushing the boundaries of human understanding and technological innovation, with the ultimate goal of improving the lives of people worldwide

OpenAI is a research organization focused on artificial intelligence (AI), and Musk's vision for it is to develop safe and beneficial AI technologies that can greatly benefit humanity. By conducting research and advocating for responsible AI development, OpenAI seeks to shape the future of AI in a way that aligns with public interest.

Neuralink, on the other hand, aims to revolutionize the field of neuroscience and develop brain-computer interfaces (BCIs) that can enhance human capabilities. Musk envisions a future where BCIs enable seamless communication between humans and machines, with possibilities ranging from treating neurological conditions to achieving symbiotic integration with AI.

6. Controversies and Challenges

6.1 Legal Battles and Public Feuds

Despite his impressive accomplishments, Elon Musk has not been immune to controversies and legal battles. His outspoken nature and sometimes impulsive behavior have landed him in hot water on several occasions.

One of the most notable instances was Musk's public feud with the United States Securities and Exchange Commission (SEC). The SEC accused Musk of securities fraud after he tweeted about potentially taking Tesla private, leading to a settlement that involved him stepping down as chairman of the company and paying a hefty fine.

Musk has also faced legal challenges related to labor practices and working conditions at Tesla factories. Critics have accused the company of not doing enough to ensure the welfare of its workers, leading to lawsuits and public scrutiny.

6.2 Production Challenges and Criticisms

While Musk's companies have achieved groundbreaking innovations, they have not been without their fair share of production challenges. Tesla, for example, has faced criticism and scrutiny over production delays and quality control issues. Meeting the high demand for Tesla vehicles has been a significant hurdle that Musk and his team are continuously working to overcome.

SpaceX has also encountered setbacks along the way. From failed rocket launches to unexpected technical difficulties, the space exploration company has had its fair share of challenges. However, these setbacks have not deterred Musk's determination to push the boundaries of space technology and achieve his ambitious goals.

It's important to note that controversies and challenges are not uncommon in the world of business and innovation. Despite these obstacles, Musk's relentless drive and ability to learn from setbacks continue to shape his journey and contribute to his growth as a visionary entrepreneur.

7. Vision for the Future

7.1 Sustainable Transportation and Renewable Energy Goals

Elon Musk is known for his steadfast commitment to creating a sustainable future. Central to his vision is the transformation of transportation and energy systems to combat climate change.

Through Tesla, Musk has been instrumental in popularizing electric vehicles and driving the transition away from fossil fuel-powered cars.

He believes that sustainable transportation is key to reducing greenhouse gas emissions and combating the environmental challenges we face. With the development of groundbreaking electric vehicles and a robust Supercharger network, Tesla has disrupted the automotive industry while paving the way for a greener future.

Beyond electric cars, Musk's vision extends to revolutionize the energy sector by accelerating the adoption of renewable energy sources. Tesla's energy division, which includes the production of solar panels and energy storage solutions, aims to create a sustainable and decentralized energy system. Musk envisions a world where homes and businesses are powered by clean energy, reducing our reliance on fossil fuels and combating climate change.

8. Legacy and Influence

8.1 Impact on Business, Technology, and Innovation

Elon Musk's impact on the business, technology, and innovation landscapes cannot be understated. He has revolutionized multiple industries, from electric vehicles to space exploration, challenging the status quo and driving industry-wide transformations.

Musk's entrepreneurial endeavors have inspired countless individuals to pursue audacious goals and think beyond traditional boundaries. His relentless pursuit of innovation, coupled with his ability to attract top talent, has propelled his companies to achieve groundbreaking advancements that were once considered science fiction.

Tesla's success has not only disrupted the automotive industry but has also spurred the acceleration of electric vehicle adoption globally. Musk's vision and determination have played a significant role in shaping the electric vehicle market and driving other automakers to invest in sustainable transportation.

SpaceX, with its achievements in reusable rocket technology and plans for interplanetary travel, has reinvigorated the space industry. By significantly reducing the cost of space launches, Musk has opened up new possibilities for scientific research, satellite deployment, and even commercial space tourism.

8.2 Inspiring the Next Generation of Entrepreneurs

Elon Musk's remarkable life and tireless pursuit of innovation have left an indelible impact on business, sustainability, space exploration, and philanthropy. From revolutionizing the electric car industry with Tesla to pioneering private space exploration with SpaceX, Musk's vision and determination have pushed the boundaries of what is possible. As he continues to inspire and challenge the status quo, it is clear that Elon Musk's legacy will be one of revolutionary advancements and a relentless pursuit of a sustainable and interplanetary future.

FAQs

1. What are some of Elon Musk's most notable business ventures?

Elon Musk is known for his involvement in several groundbreaking ventures. Some of his most notable business ventures include Tesla Motors, SpaceX, Neuralink, and The Boring Company.

2. How has Elon Musk contributed to sustainability and clean energy?

Musk has been a strong advocate for sustainable technology and clean energy. He co-founded SolarCity, now a part of Tesla, which specializes in solar energy solutions. Additionally, Musk's Tesla Motors has played a crucial role in advancing the adoption of electric vehicles, with a focus on reducing reliance on fossil fuels.

3. What are some of Elon Musk's achievements in the space industry?

Musk's space exploration company, SpaceX, has achieved several milestones. Notable achievements include the successful development and launch of the Falcon 1, Falcon 9, and Falcon Heavy rockets, as well as Dragon spacecraft. SpaceX's accomplishments also include becoming the first privately-funded company to send a spacecraft to the International Space Station (ISS). You did not mention the Falcon rockets above and "rockets" sounds like both defensive and offensive weaponry. Consider clarifying what these are and their purpose(s).

4. How has Elon Musk contributed to philanthropy and social impact initiatives?

Musk has made significant contributions to philanthropy and social impact initiatives. Through the Musk Foundation, he has supported various causes, including education, renewable energy research, and humanitarian efforts. Additionally, Musk has co-founded organizations such as OpenAI and Neuralink, which aim to advance artificial intelligence (AI) research and brain-computer interfaces (BCI), respectively, for the betterment of society.

Elon Musk's Rules for Succes

Really like what you do.

- **Don't listen to the little man.** We're doing these things which seem unlikely to succeed and we've been fortunate that at least thus far they have succeeded.

- **Never give up.** I'd have to be dead or completely incapacitated to give up."

- **Take a risk:** Take risks now and do something bold, you won't regret it.

- **Do something important:** If something is important enough you should try even if the probable outcome is failure.

- **Focus on signal over noise:** Focus on 'signal over noise'…Are these efforts that people are undergoing resulting in a better product or service? If they're not, stop those efforts.

- **Look for problem solvers:** When interviewing somebody to work in a company, ask them, 'Tell me about the problems you worked on and how did you solve them?' and if someone was really the person who solved the problems, they'd be able to answer at multiple levels, and if they weren't, they'd get stuck. It's really important to like what you do if you don't like it, life is too short."

- **Attract great people:** All a company is, is a group of people that create a problem or service and so dependent on how talented or hard working that group is and the degree to which they are focused cohesively in a good direction that will determine the success of a company.

- **Have a great product:** You're always going to buy the trusted brand unless there's a big difference. A lot of times an entrepreneur will come up with something that is just slightly better, and it can't just be slightly better, it's got to be a lot better.

- Don't just follow the trend: If you look at all of Elon's businesses, they solve huge problems in emerging markets where there is little competition. When he co-founded PayPal they were, for a time, the only email money transferring solution in the world.

SpaceX is the first private company to send a spacecraft (Dragon) to the ISS. Tesla is the world's leading electric car company. In his USC commencement speech, Elon recommends, "Don't just follow the trend," and his actions have certainly followed this advice.

- Focus on innovation rather than competition. Strive to innovate to such a degree that there are no competitors. Elon's Billionaire business partner Peter Thiel writes on this topic in his book Zero to One, If you want to create and capture lasting value, look to innovate and create a monopoly.

- **Monopolies by definition transcend competition and are how the greatest business profits can be achieved.**

- Work super hard: "If you do the simple math, if somebody else is working 50 hours and you are working 100, you'll get twice as much done in the course of a year as the other company."

- **Don't Fear Failure:** In an interview, Musk has stated that he originally thought Tesla would fail. When asked why he would start a company that he didn't think would be successful his answer was: "If something is important enough you should try even if the probable outcome is failure." Elon wanted to get rid of the perception that electric cars are ugly and slow.

Although entirely changing the way the public perceives a product class is no easy task Musk has made it happen. The Tesla Model S sedan topped Consumer Reports' annual customer satisfaction ratings two years in a row.

- **Be Ready to Learn New Skills:** Don't let what you don't know stop you from tackling important endeavors.

Musk never owned a car company before, but that didn't stop him from starting Tesla.

Musk was never a rocket scientist, but that didn't stop him from starting SpaceX.

There are plenty of books out there and there is more information readily available than ever before so set your sights high because there is plenty of information online about how you can make it happen.

- **Seek Out Constructive Criticism:** In an interview with Elon Musk below he touches on several of his success secrets that I share in this post.

One success tip that many people likely avoid is seeking out criticism. No one likes hearing what they are potentially doing wrong but by seeking out this information from people you trust you gain valuable insight that you may be able to use to make improvements.

I think it's important for people to pay close attention to negative feedback and rather than ignore negative feedback, you have to listen to it carefully.

Ignore it if the underlying reason for the negative feedback doesn't make sense but otherwise, people should adjust their behavior.

I'm not perfect at it, for sure, but I do think it's really important to solicit negative feedback, particularly from people who have your best interest in mind.

- **Be Unrelentingly Optimistic:** Musk is known for setting impossible deadlines and making requests of his employees to cut costs by up to 90%. A lot of the time these deadlines fail, but often they succeed.

With the optimism to tackle massive goals you can often achieve success even if you fall a bit short of your original target. Challenge yourself to think big and this will often yield big returns. Seeking unreasonable levels of success is a strategy that can lead you to exceptional success.

- **Start From First Principles:** In his interview with Kevin Rose, Musk explains his thoughts about reasoning up from first principles. "Boil things down to the most fundamental truths. Then reason up from there."

- **Strive to Be Significantly Better Than The Competition:** Put yourself in the shoes of the consumer, Musk says. "They are going to buy the trusted brand unless there is a big difference." So if you want to set yourself apart from the competition, don't just try to be a bit better. Strive to be *significantly* better.

- **Be Extremely Tenacious:** Here is a definition Google gave me for the word Tenacious: Adjective Not readily relinquishing a position, principle, or course of action; determined.

The determination to keep going when the going gets tough is what saved SpaceX and Tesla when both were on the verge of bankruptcy. Musk poured all of his money from the sale of PayPal into these companies so they could survive and his tenacity in doing so saved them from insolvency. The perseverance and hard work Musk has shown in making every company he has worked with a success reminds me of this quote from Steve Jobs: "I'm convinced that about half of what separates the successful entrepreneurs from the non-successful ones is pure perseverance."

- **Focus on a High Value Pursuit:** A strategy Musk recommends is focusing on building a business in which you are confident will have a high value for others. Being rigorous and real in your self-analysis will help keep you grounded and on the path to success.

- **Consider The Worst-Case Scenario:** When Musk decided he wanted to be an entrepreneur at 17 years old, he forced himself to live off $1 per day. At that time, he lived mainly off hot dogs and oranges. He stated, "I figured if I could live off a dollar a day, then at least from a food standpoint, it's pretty easy to earn $30 a month."

Musk didn't do it because he was poor. He did it to see if he had what it took to lead the life of an entrepreneur. Since he was successful with this experiment, he knew that money wouldn't be an issue.

By experimenting with what it actually felt to be poor he realized he could do it if he had to.

- **Invest Profits Into New Businesses:** Both times Musk cashed in a company for millions of dollars, he invested at least 45% of his earnings back into a brand new business within the calendar year. $10 million of the $22 million Musk made from the sale of Zip2 went to founding X.com (later PayPal). $100 million of the $165 million he made from the sale of PayPal went to founding SpaceX.

- **Know Your Limits:** Musk may be the smartest and hardest working entrepreneur of the 21st century – but he still only has 24 hours in a day. Musk also has a wife and five boys who undoubtedly want time with him as well.

  Although Musk was ambitious enough to take on the challenge of SpaceX and Tesla at the same time, he realized that another major project would be too much to manage.

  Back in 2006, Musk had an idea for a solar panel company, but he knew if he started it he would have too much on the go. So, he shared his idea with his cousins Peter and Lyndon Rive, who founded SolarCity with Musk as the principle investor. Musk has served as chairman of the board since its inception, but he's kept enough distance so that it doesn't eat up too much of his time and energy.

- **Have Out of This World Ambition:** Musk's ambition is to colonize Mars as a way to back up the human race. Colonizing Mars is much more than a business decision for Musk; it's about the future of the human species: "I think it's important that humanity become a multi-planet species. I think most people would agree that a future where we are a spacefaring civilization is inspiring and exciting compared with one where we are forever confined to Earth until some eventual extinction event. That's really why I started SpaceX."

  In Ashlee Vance's biography of Musk, Elon reveals that he wishes to establish a Mars colony by 2040, with a population of 80,000.

Create a World Class Work Environment: Most car factories are dark and gloomy. Tesla takes a different approach. The Tesla factory was inspired by the SpaceX work environment and features light paint and natural light.

- **Let Your Imagination Soar:** With awe-inspiring ideas which aim to transform today into future, this innovator has enjoyed first mover advantage in all his business ventures.

Elon Musk has generated a massive amount of press for himself with his highly imaginative idea the Hyperloop. The Hyperloop is Musk's proposal for a faster new form of transportation between the Greater Los Angeles Area and the San Francisco Bay Area.

The system is proposed to use a partial vacuum to reduce aerodynamic drag, which it is theorized would allow for high-speed travel with relatively low power.

Constantly Improve.

Musk said that the single best piece of advice he can give is: "Constantly think about how you can be doing things better"

Innovation and Success Quotes

"I think it is possible for ordinary people to choose to be extraordinary."

Elon Musk's willingness to publicly discuss even the failures of his insanely ambitious SpaceX missions reminds us just how confident the man truly is. Musk has accomplished feats previously thought impossible--in fact, if he'd listened to his advisers, he'd never have experienced the success he has. Born in South Africa in 1971, he sold his first computer game at age 12 and went on to co-found Tesla Motors, PayPal and SpaceX.

Elon Musk is a risk taker; he's an innovator and dares to dream the big dreams. Further, he has the ability to actually make them happen.

He's kind of a badass. How does he do it? I'm a huge advocate of learning from the experience and wisdom of others, and this man is so extraordinarily successful and intelligent that we'd be fools not to listen to him. See what you can learn from these innovation and success quotes from Elon Musk:

- When something is important enough, you do it even if the odds are not in your favor.

- Some people don't like change, but you need to embrace change if the alternative is disaster.

- Failure is an option here. If things are not failing, you are not innovating enough.

- The path to the CEO's office should not be through the CFO's office, and it should not be through the marketing department. It needs to be through engineering and design.

- Persistence is very important. You should not give up unless you are forced to give up.

- I think it's very important to have a feedback loop, where you're constantly thinking about what you've done and how you could be doing it better.

- There's a tremendous bias against taking risks. Everyone is trying to optimize their ass-covering.

- It's OK to have your eggs in one basket as long as you control what happens to that basket.

- Brand is just a perception, and perception will match reality over time. Sometimes it will be ahead, other times it will be behind. But brand is simply a collective impression some have about a product.

- I don't think it's a good idea to plan to sell a company.

- It is a mistake to hire huge numbers of people to get a complicated job done. Numbers will never compensate for talent in getting the right answer (two people who don't know something are no better than one), will tend to slow down progress, and will make the task incredibly expensive."

- "A company is a group organized to create a product or service, and it is only as good as its people and how excited they are about creating. I do want to recognize a ton of super-talented people. I just happen to be the face of the companies.

- People work better when they know what the goal is and why. It is important that people look forward to coming to work in the morning and enjoy working.

- If you're co-founder or CEO, you have to do all kinds of tasks you might not want to do... If you don't do your chores, the company won't succeed... No task is too menial.

- I say something, and then it usually happens. Maybe not on schedule, but it usually happens.

- I do think there is a lot of potential if you have a compelling product and people are willing to pay a premium for that. I think that is what Apple has shown. You can buy a much cheaper cell phone or laptop, but Apple's product is so much better than the alternative, and people are willing to pay that premium.

- I don't spend my time pontificating about high-concept things; I spend my time solving engineering and manufacturing problems.

- I always invest my own money in the companies that I create. I don't believe in the whole thing of just using other people's money. I don't think that's right. I'm not going to ask other people to invest in something if I'm not prepared to do so myself.

- My biggest mistake is probably weighing too much on someone's talent and not someone's personality. I think it matters whether someone has a good heart.

- I don't create companies for the sake of creating companies, but to get things done.

- I don't believe in process. In fact, when I interview a potential employee and he or she says that 'it's all about the process,' I see that as a bad sign. The problem is that at a lot of big companies, process becomes a substitute for thinking. You're encouraged to behave like a little gear in a complex machine. Frankly, it allows you to keep people who aren't that smart, who aren't that creative.

- Starting and growing a business is as much about the innovation, drive, and determination of the people behind it as the product they sell.

- The first step is to establish that something is possible; then probability will occur.

- There are really two things that have to occur in order for a new technology to be affordable to the mass market. One is you need economies of scale. The other is you need to iterate on the design. You need to go through a few versions.

- Talent is extremely important. It's like a sports team; the team that has the best individual player will often win, but then there's a multiplier from how those players work together and the strategy they employ.

- Work like hell. I mean you just have to put in 80-to-100-hour weeks every week. [This] improves the odds of success. If other people are putting in 40-hour workweeks and you're putting in 100-hour workweeks, then even if you're doing the same thing, you know that you will achieve in four months what it takes them a year to achieve.

- I've actually not read any books on time management.

- I'm interested in things that change the world or that affect the future and wondrous, new technology where you see it, and you're like, 'Wow, how did that even happen? How is that possible?'

- Really pay attention to negative feedback and solicit it, particularly from friends. ... Hardly anyone does that, and it's incredibly helpful.

- If you get up in the morning and think the future is going to be better, it is a bright day. Otherwise, it's not.

- Good ideas are always crazy until they're not

- What makes innovative thinking happen?... I think it's really a mindset. You have to decide.

- People should pursue what they're passionate about. That will make them happier than pretty much anything else.

- Being an entrepreneur is like eating glass and staring into the abyss of death.

- I wouldn't say I have a lack of fear. In fact, I'd like my fear emotion to be less because it's very distracting and fries my nervous system.

- If you're trying to create a company, it's like baking a cake. You have to have all the ingredients in the right proportion.

- I think most of the important stuff on the Internet has been built. There will be continued innovation, for sure, but the great problems of the Internet have essentially been solved.

- I think we have a duty to maintain the light of consciousness to make sure it continues into the future.

- When Henry Ford made cheap, reliable cars, people said, 'Nah, what's wrong with a horse?' That was a huge bet he made, and it worked.

- When somebody has a breakthrough innovation, it is rarely one little thing. Very rarely, is it one little thing. It's usually a whole bunch of things that collectively amount to a huge innovation.

- You shouldn't do things differently just because they're different. They need to be... better.

- You have to say, 'Well, why did it succeed where others did not?'

- I would just question things... It would infuriate my parents... That I wouldn't just believe them when they said something 'cause I'd ask them why. And then I'd consider whether that response made sense, given everything else I knew.

- It's very important to like the people you work with, otherwise life [and] your job is gonna be quite miserable.

- We have a strict 'no-assholes policy' at SpaceX.

- I think the best way to attract venture capital is to try and come up with a demonstration of whatever product or service it is and ideally take that as far as you can. Just see if you can sell that to real customers and start generating some momentum. The further along you can get with that, the more likely you are to get funding.

- Disruptive technology where you really have a big technology discontinuity... tends to come from new companies.

- As much as possible, avoid hiring MBAs. MBA programs don't teach people how to create companies.

- Don't delude yourself into thinking something's working when it's not, or you're gonna get fixated on a bad solution.

- If something has to be designed and invented, and you have to figure out how to ensure that the value of the thing you create is greater than the cost of the inputs, then that is probably my core skill.

- I always have optimism, but I'm realistic. It was not with the expectation of great success that I started Tesla or SpaceX... It's just that I thought they were important enough to do anyway.

Sources: Corecom Consulting, https://www.corecomconsulting.co.uk/elon-10-rules-for-success/. June 27, 2021.

Garin Kilpatrick, https://garinkilpatrick.com/elon-musk/ June 27, 2021.

LAFFAZ, https://laffaz.com/motivational-elon-musk-quotes/. June 27, 2021.

Chapter 6

SUCCESS RULES FROM ALIKO DANGOTE, AFRICA'S TOP BILLIONAIRE

Aliko Dangote – His Life and Contributions. An Introduction

Aliko Dangote, widely regarded as one of Africa's most prominent businessmen, has achieved remarkable success through his entrepreneurial ventures and philanthropic efforts. Born and raised in Nigeria, Dangote's journey from humble beginnings to becoming the richest person in Africa is an inspiring tale of determination, innovation, and resilience. This article delves into the life and contributions of Aliko Dangote, exploring his early years, the establishment of his business empire under the Dangote Group, his immense impact on the African economy and industry, as well as his notable philanthropic initiatives. Furthermore, it examines the valuable lessons that can be learned from his remarkable success story, while also addressing the challenges and controversies that have accompanied his rise to prominence. Ultimately, this article highlights the enduring legacy and profound impact of Aliko Dangote on Africa's business landscape and social development.

1. Introduction: Aliko Dangote - A Brief Biography

Meet Aliko Dangote, one of Africa's most influential and wealthiest individuals. Born on April 10, 1957, in Kano, Nigeria, Dangote has built an empire that spans various industries and has made significant contributions to the continent's economy. Let's delve into his early life, education, business ventures, and his remarkable impact on Africa.

1.Early Life and Family Background

Dangote was born into a wealthy family; his grandfather, Sanusi Dantata, was one of the wealthiest men in West Africa at the time. Growing up, he witnessed the entrepreneurial spirit of his grandfather and was inspired to follow in his footsteps.

1.1 Education and Early Career

Despite his family's affluence, Dangote was determined to carve his own path and make his mark. He attended Sheikh Ali Kumasi Madaki Primary School and then proceeded to Capital High School in Kano. After completing his education, he enrolled in the Al-Azhar University in Cairo, Egypt, to study Business.

After returning from Egypt, Dangote started his professional journey by working for his uncle's company, but soon realized that he desired more than just a salaried job. He set his sights on establishing his own business empire.

2. Early Life and Education

2.1 Family Background and Upbringing

Aliko Dangote's childhood was filled with privilege, but it was also shaped by the entrepreneurial legacy of his family. With his grandfather's success as a prominent businessman, he grew up witnessing the rewards of hard work and determination.

2.2 Educational Journey and Academic Achievements

Dangote's educational path laid a solid foundation for his future success. He completed his early education in Nigeria before pursuing further studies abroad. At Al-Azhar University in Cairo, Egypt, he honed his business acumen and gained invaluable knowledge that would serve him well in his entrepreneurial endeavors.

Throughout his academic journey, Dangote demonstrated a remarkable dedication to learning and achieving excellence. His academic achievements were the stepping stones to his future accomplishments.

3. Building an Empire: Dangote Group and Business Ventures

3.1 Founding of Dangote Group

In 1977, at the age of 21, Dangote founded the Dangote Group, a trading firm that focused on commodities such as cement, sugar, and flour. He started small but had big ambitions, and his relentless drive propelled the company's growth over the years.

3.2 Diversification and Expansion of Business Interests

Dangote's business acumen and forward-thinking approach led him to diversify his business interests. The Dangote Group expanded into sectors such as manufacturing, telecommunications, real estate, and oil refining. This strategic decision enabled him to capitalize on the vast opportunities in the African market.

3.3 Milestones and Achievements

Over the years, Dangote has achieved numerous milestones that have solidified his status as a business mogul. He has consistently been listed as one of the richest individuals in Africa and globally, amassing a fortune through his various ventures. Additionally, his companies have contributed significantly to job creation and economic growth in the countries where they operate.

4. Aliko Dangote's Contributions to African Economy and Industry

4.1 Creating Job Opportunities and Economic Growth

Dangote's businesses have played a pivotal role in creating job opportunities across Africa. Through his ventures, he has provided employment to thousands of individuals, helping to alleviate poverty and improve livelihoods. His commitment to hiring and empowering local talent has had a profound impact on the economies of the countries where his companies operate.

4.2 Promoting Local Industries and Manufacturing

Dangote has been a strong advocate for developing local industries and reducing Africa's dependence on imports. His investments in cement production, sugar refining, and other manufacturing sectors have bolstered domestic production capacities and reduced the need for imports. By promoting local industries, he has contributed to the growth and sustainability of African economies.

4.3 Investments in Infrastructure and Agriculture

Recognizing the importance of infrastructure and agriculture in Africa's development, Dangote has directed substantial investments toward these sectors. His endeavors include the construction of cement plants, ports, and roads, which have improved connectivity and facilitated trade within the continent. Furthermore, his agricultural initiatives have aimed to enhance food security and promote agricultural sustainability.

5. Philanthropic Initiatives: Aliko Dangote's Commitment to Social Development

5.1 Overview of Dangote Foundation

When it comes to giving back, Aliko Dangote doesn't hold back. Through his Dangote Foundation, he has established himself as a leading philanthropist in Africa. The foundation focuses on improving the lives of Nigerians and Africans at large, with a particular emphasis on education, healthcare, and poverty alleviation. Dangote's dedication to social development is truly commendable.

5.2 Supporting Education and Healthcare

One of the areas where Dangote's philanthropy shines is education. He understands that education is the bedrock of development, and he has invested heavily in ensuring that young Africans have access to quality education. From building primary schools in rural areas to providing scholarships for higher education, Dangote is actively working toward creating a brighter future for the continent.

In addition to education, Dangote has also made significant contributions to the healthcare sector. He has invested in medical facilities and programs aimed at improving healthcare access and quality. His efforts in combating diseases like malaria and HIV/AIDS have had a profound impact on the lives of many Africans.

5.3 Humanitarian Aid and Disaster Relief

Dangote's philanthropic efforts extend beyond education and healthcare. In times of crisis, he has stepped up to provide humanitarian aid and disaster relief. Whether it's helping communities affected by natural disasters or supporting refugees, Dangote has consistently shown his commitment to alleviating human suffering.

6. Lessons from Aliko Dangote's Success Story

6.1 Entrepreneurial Mindset and Determination

Aliko Dangote's success story is a testament to the power of having an entrepreneurial mindset and staying determined in the face of challenges. From his early days as a trader to building an empire in sectors like cement, sugar, and oil, Dangote's journey is an inspiration to aspiring entrepreneurs. He has always been willing to take calculated risks and seize opportunities, proving that a strong vision and unwavering determination can lead to extraordinary achievements.

6.2 Importance of Innovation and Adaptability

Dangote's constant pursuit of innovation and adaptability are key attributes of his success. He understands the importance of staying ahead of the curve and continuously evolving with the changing business landscape. Whether it's adopting new technologies or diversifying his business interests, Dangote's ability to adapt has been instrumental in his achievements.

6.3 Building Strong Networks and Partnerships

No one achieves greatness alone, and Dangote understands this well. He has built a vast network of influential contacts and has been successful in forming strategic partnerships. By leveraging these relationships, he has been able to expand his business ventures, gain access to new markets, and make a greater impact through his philanthropic efforts. Dangote's ability to build strong networks is a valuable lesson in the world of business.

7. Challenges and Controversies: A Candid Look at Dangote's Journey

7.1 Managing Business Risks and Economic Volatility

Despite his phenomenal success, Dangote's journey has not been without challenges. Like any entrepreneur, he has had to navigate through economic downturns, fluctuations in commodity prices, and regulatory hurdles. His ability to manage risks and maneuver through volatile business environments has allowed him to emerge stronger and more resilient.

7.2 Environmental Concerns and Sustainability

As a prominent figure in industries like cement and oil, Dangote has faced criticisms regarding environmental concerns and sustainability practices. While these concerns should not be ignored, it is important to note that Dangote has taken steps to address these issues. His commitment to community development, education, and healthcare also showcases his dedication to overall sustainability.

7.3 Public Perception and Criticisms

As one of Africa's richest individuals, Dangote is no stranger to public scrutiny. His wealth and influence have made him a target for criticisms and envy. It is essential to recognize that his success is a product of hard work, determination, and genuine efforts to make a positive impact on society. It is important not to let baseless criticisms overshadow his significant contributions.

8. Aliko Dangote's Legacy and Impact on Africa

8.1 Legacy of Success and Inspiration

Aliko Dangote's remarkable journey from a small trader to one of Africa's wealthiest individuals is a testament to what one can achieve with perseverance, innovation, and a commitment to social responsibility. His success story is an inspiration to millions of Africans who aspire to create their own path to greatness.

8.2 Continued Influence on African Business and Philanthropy

Dangote's impact goes far beyond his personal achievements. His business empire has created numerous job opportunities, driving economic growth and development across Africa. Moreover, his steadfast commitment to philanthropy and social development serves as a model for other African entrepreneurs, encouraging them to use their success to uplift their communities. Aliko Dangote's legacy will continue to shape the future of African business and philanthropy for generations to come.

9. Conclusion: Aliko Dangote's Legacy and Impact on Africa

In conclusion, Aliko Dangote's life and contributions serve as a shining example of what can be achieved through determination, hard work, and a commitment to making a positive impact. From his humble beginnings to building a vast business empire, Dangote has not only transformed industries and economies, but also has demonstrated a deep sense of social responsibility through his philanthropic endeavors. His story inspires aspiring entrepreneurs across Africa and beyond, reminding us that success is attainable with a clear vision, innovation, and a willingness to overcome challenges. Aliko Dangote's legacy will continue to shape Africa's future, leaving an indelible mark on the continent's business landscape and serving as a beacon of hope for generations to come.

FAQs

1. What is Aliko Dangote's net worth?

Aliko Dangote's net worth fluctuates due to market conditions, but as of this writing , his estimated net worth is around $11.4 billion, making him one of the wealthiest individuals in Africa and globally.

2. How has Aliko Dangote contributed to economic growth in Africa?

Aliko Dangote has made significant contributions to economic growth in Africa through his diverse business ventures. His investments in industries such as cement, sugar, and agriculture have created job opportunities, stimulated local economies, and promoted self-sufficiency in vital sectors across the continent.

3. What philanthropic initiatives has Aliko Dangote undertaken?

Aliko Dangote is known for his philanthropic efforts through the Dangote Foundation. The foundation focuses on improving education, healthcare, and poverty alleviation in Nigeria and other African countries. Dangote has generously donated to various causes, including scholarships, medical centers, and disaster relief efforts.

4. What lessons can be learned from Aliko Dangote's success?

Aliko Dangote's success offers several valuable lessons. His unwavering determination, ability to adapt to changing market conditions, emphasis on innovation, and commitment to building strong networks and partnerships have been instrumental in his achievements. Additionally, his emphasis on investing in local industries and giving back to society highlights the importance of social responsibility in business endeavors.

Aliko Dangote's Success Rules:

- **Listen to people**: If you want to be a good leader, you have to listen to people and value team work

- **Be consistent**: Life without challenges is very boring. Just because you have hiccups in business doesn't mean you should quit.

- **Possess the right information**: Having the right information helps you make the right decisions

- **Be focused:** Be dedicated. Don't take your business or your job as something you must do; rather take it as a hobby (something you enjoy) and you will do better at it

- **Think ahead**

- **Have a vision:** For an entrepreneur there are no boundaries. You can excel far beyond your expectations. But you must have a vision and a mission to excel. Three to five years ago I never expected to be on *Forbes'* list.

- **Do only things you understand:** Any business I don't understand, I don't do. That's why we are successful

- **Think big:** Be bold and be ready to take calculated risks, not just any risk. If you think small, you will always remain small.

- **Form strategic plans:** Have a strategy for how you will achieve your vision

- **Your name is your most valuable asset:** Be honest and don't destroy your name. It doesn't matter how big you are; if you have a bad name no one will touch you.

Inspiring Aliko Dangote Quotes

- I enjoy myself a lot but I derive more joy in working. I believe in hard work and one of my business success secrets is hard work. It's hard to see a youth that will go to bed by 2am and wake up by 5am. I don't rest until I achieve something

- Every morning when I wake up, I make up my mind to solve as many problems [as possible] before retiring home.

- When you have made it in life, you must give back to those who made you.

- My grandfather once told me, the soul of business is not making money but making people happy.

- To succeed in business, you must build a brand and never destroy it.

- In whatever you do, strive to be the best at it.

- You could easily tell that hard work and perseverance go hand in hand with patience. We often hear people say patience is worth it, yet we don't practice it. I did and look how well it worked out for me.

- Don't kill the competition. Competition is healthy for businesses. It keeps you, the entrepreneur, on your toes.

- Motivation, backed by good planning and correct action, leads to success.

- Endeavor to work as hard as possible to attain a new aim with each day that comes by. Don't go to bed until you have achieved something productive.

- Passion is what drives me forward. Passion is what makes me go to bed at 2 a.m. and wake up 6 a.m.

- If you don't have ambition, you shouldn't be alive.

- If I had challenges in my company, I would not hesitate to sell assets to remain afloat, to get to the better times, because it doesn't make any sense for me to keep any assets and then suffocate the whole organization.

- The most dangerous thing for an entrepreneur to do is to actually go into a business that he does not understand fully.

- I always make sure I hire people smarter than me.

- I always tried to move up the food chain. I started with cement and then moved into textiles and banking. When I was trading sugar, I added salt and flour so that then we could do pasta. And then I thought, why not make the bag for it, too? So, we started making packaging.

- What I always say is that money doesn't have color. It doesn't matter whether you are from Africa or anywhere in the world. The color of money is the same.

- I built a conglomerate and emerged the richest black man in the world in 2008, but it didn't happen overnight. It took me thirty years to get to where I am today. Youths of today aspire to be like me, but they want to achieve it overnight. It's not going to work. To build a successful business, you must start small and dream big. In the journey of entrepreneurship, tenacity of purpose is supreme.

- After my death, I want to be remembered as Africa's greatest industrialist.

- Manufacture, don't just trade. There is money in manufacturing even though it is capital- intensive. To achieve a big breakthrough, I had to start manufacturing the same product I was trading on, which is commodities.

- If people look inward, they would see the opportunities for greatness

- When you import goods, you import poverty and you export jobs to other parts of the globe where such goods are produced.

- Exercise is better than any medicine I can take; exercise and sleep.

- Invest now, before it's too late. The train is about to leave the station.

- The real thing about wealth, what will make you enjoy it and be happy that, yes, you are rich, is how many lives you can touch while you are alive.

- You must have a vision and not just a vision, but you must have a plan that would make you fulfil that vision

Source: The Success Elite, https://thesuccesselite.com/top-30-aliko-dangote-quotes-on-being-a-successful-entrepreneur/ June 27, 2021. All rights reserved.

The inspire series, http://inspiredbyglory.com/aliko-dangotes-10-rules-for-success/ June 27, 2021. All rights reserved

Chapter 7

ROBERT F. SMITH'S SUCCESS RULES

An Introduction to Robert F. Smith: His Life and Contributions

Robert F. Smith is a prominent figure whose life and accomplishments make a significant impact across various fields. From his humble beginnings to becoming one of the most influential business leaders of our time, Smith's journey is nothing short of inspiring. This article delves into his early life and education; highlights his successful business ventures; explores his contributions to the tech and finance industries; examines his philanthropic endeavors and initiatives and draws insights from the valuable lessons he has learned along the way. Join us as we unravel the story of Robert F. Smith and discover the profound impact he has made through his biography, life, business, contributions, philanthropy, and lessons.

1. Early Life and Education

1.1 Childhood and Family Background

Robert F. Smith, a man with a name that sounds more like a civil engineer than a billionaire businessman, had a rather ordinary childhood. Born in Denver, Colorado on December 1, 1962, and raised in a modest family, he learned the value of hard work and perseverance from an early age. His parents imbued him with the importance of education and a strong sense of ambition.

1.2 Educational Journey and Academic Achievements

Smith's educational journey was nothing short of impressive. He attended a local public high school where he excelled academically and discovered his passion for mathematics and finance. Armed with an insatiable curiosity, he went on to pursue a degree in chemical engineering at Cornell University, but life had other plans for him. After realizing that his true calling lay in the world of finance, Smith switched gears and earned his MBA from Columbia Business School. This decision would shape his career trajectory, leading him to become one of the most successful investors and business moguls of our time.

2. Career and Business Ventures

2.1 Early Career and Professional Development

Like many ambitious individuals, Smith started his career by working for established firms in the finance industry. He honed his skills at companies like Goldman Sachs and later became an esteemed investment banker at the renowned investment firm, Kraft Group.

2.2 Entrepreneurial Ventures and Business Successes

In 2000, Smith's entrepreneurial spirit eventually led him to establish his own private equity firm, Vista Equity Partners., Under his leadership, the firm experienced tremendous growth and success, specializing in investing in software and technology companies. Today, Vista Equity Partners manages over $70 billion in assets, making Smith one of the wealthiest individuals in the world.

3. Contributions to the Tech and Finance Industries

3.1 Influence and Impact in the Technology Sector

Smith's contributions to the technology sector have been groundbreaking. His visionary approach and understanding of the industry have led to numerous innovations and advancements in software and technology companies. Through Vista Equity Partners, he has helped transform struggling tech companies into major players in their respective fields.

3.2 Innovations and Breakthroughs in Finance

In addition to his impact on the technology sector, Smith also has made significant breakthroughs in finance. He introduced unique investment strategies that have revolutionized the private equity industry. His expertise and ability to identify lucrative investment opportunities have earned him a reputation as a savvy investor and business leader.

4. Philanthropic Endeavors and Initiatives

4.1 Overview of Philanthropic Philosophy

Beyond his immense success in the business world, Robert F. Smith is also known for his philanthropy. He firmly believes in giving back and has made it his mission to address pressing societal issues. With a passion for education, he focuses on providing opportunities and support to underprivileged communities, offering scholarships and grants to talented students.

4.2 Key Philanthropic Initiatives and Organizations Supported

Smith's philanthropic initiatives include his generous donation to Morehouse College, where he pledged to pay off the student loan debt of the entire graduating class. This act of kindness not only alleviated the financial burden for many graduates, but also highlighted the importance of investing in education and empowering future generations. In addition, he has actively supported organizations that promote equality and social justice, such as the National Museum of African American History and Culture.

5. Lessons Learned and Leadership Principles

Robert F. Smith's life and achievements offer valuable lessons to aspiring entrepreneurs and individuals alike. From his humble beginnings to his extraordinary success, he exemplifies the power of hard work, perseverance, and the ability to adapt to changing circumstances. His commitment to philanthropy reminds us of the importance of giving back and using our success to make a positive impact on the world. So let's take a page from Smith's book and dare to dream big, work hard, and make a difference in everything we do.

5.1 Personal and Professional Development Insights

When it comes to personal and professional development, Robert F. Smith has some valuable insights to offer. One lesson he emphasizes is the importance of continuous learning. Smith believes that growth doesn't stop after college or once you land a prestigious job. Instead, he encourages individuals to invest in their own education, whether it's through attending seminars, reading books, or seeking out mentors. Smith himself is known for his voracious appetite for knowledge, and for constantly seeking new opportunities to learn and grow.

Another key lesson from Smith's journey is the value of resilience. In the face of challenges and setbacks, he has always found a way to persevere. Smith believes that setbacks are merely temporary roadblocks on the path to success. It's about picking yourself up, learning from the experience, and making necessary adjustments. He encourages individuals to embrace failure as a learning opportunity and to approach challenges with a positive mindset.

5.2 Leadership Principles and Strategies for Success

Robert F. Smith's success as a leader can be attributed to several key principles and strategies. First, he believes in the power of authenticity. Smith encourages leaders to be true to themselves and to lead with integrity. By staying true to his values and principles, he has been able to inspire trust and loyalty from those around him.

Another important principle in Smith's leadership approach is the ability to create a shared vision. He believes that a strong leader should be able to articulate a clear and compelling vision that motivates others to join in the pursuit of a common goal. Smith's ability to inspire and rally people around a shared purpose has been instrumental to his success.

Additionally, Smith emphasizes the importance of building strong relationships and networks. He believes that strong connections with others can open doors and create opportunities. Smith encourages leaders to invest time and effort into building genuine relationships, and to always be open to learning from others.

Robert F. Smith's personal and professional development insights, along with his leadership principles and strategies for success, offer valuable lessons for anyone looking to grow and succeed in their own lives. Continuous learning, resilience, authenticity, shared vision, and building strong relationships are all key ingredients in his recipe for success. So, let's embrace these lessons and apply them to our own journeys, while also remembering to make room for humor and a little bit of wit along the way!

In conclusion, Robert F. Smith's remarkable biography serves as a testament to the power of determination, innovation, and philanthropy. From his early days to his extraordinary success in the business world, Smith's story is one of resilience and leadership. Through his contributions to the tech and finance industries, as well as his unwavering commitment to philanthropy, Smith has left an indelible mark on society. Moreover, his journey offers invaluable lessons on personal and professional growth, reminding us of the importance of hard work, generosity, and making a positive impact. Robert F. Smith's life and legacy continue to inspire others to strive for greatness and create a better world.

FAQs

1. What are some notable philanthropic initiatives supported by Robert F. Smith?

Robert F. Smith has been involved in numerous philanthropic initiatives. Some notable examples include his $34 million donation to the Morehouse College Class of 2019, the establishment of the Fund II Foundation to support education, environmental conservation, and human rights, and his contributions to organizations such as the Smithsonian National Museum of African American History and Culture.

2. How did Robert F. Smith make his mark in the tech and finance industries?

Robert F. Smith made significant contributions to the tech and finance industries through his leadership and innovations. As the founder and CEO of Vista Equity Partners, he pioneered the concept of enterprise software investing, revolutionizing the private equity industry. Additionally, Smith has been actively involved in investing in and supporting tech startups, further driving innovation and growth in the sector.

3. What are some key leadership principles and lessons we can learn from Robert F. Smith?

Robert F. Smith's journey offers valuable insights into leadership. Some key principles to learn from him include the importance of embracing challenges and persevering in the face of adversity; the significance of continuous learning and personal development; the power of giving back to the community, and the necessity of fostering strong relationships and collaboration in achieving success.

3. What is Robert F. Smith's net worth?

Rober Smith's net worth as at the time of writing (2023) is estimated at $9.22 billion USD.

Success Rules from Robert F. Smith

1. I'm here to tell you that, by virtue of your being here today, by virtue of walking across that stage – you are enough. (Source – Commencement Address at AU)

2. Use your skills, your knowledge, your instincts to serve – to go change the world in the way that only you can.

3. You got to have grit. And grit means getting turned away from thing 14, 16 times, calling someone every two weeks, every day for 5 months, and then finally it materializing in something that you want.

4. This is the first time in history you can create wealth and not have access to capital. You just need intellectual property. A blogger who has a large audience can create wealth by attracting advertisers.

5. Intelligence can create huge profits, and in fact, you can actually make more money being smart than you can being strong or fast. (Source – Youth Symposium)

6. Every day I need you to set a new goal.

7. The importance of developing intellectual property cannot be underestimated.

8. You are enough to be who you want to be and to create what you want to create.

9. Put action to support the intention; don't say I want to be a millionaire but then [not] take the activities to do it.

10. Have the vision of what you want to become, but you have to put consistent action behind that vision in order for that to manifest, and it as to be consistent.

11. If you get too much help you never really figure out how to do things and you don't develop the grit.

12. Fight through those problems.

13. If you can't solve easy problems now, you will not be able to solve difficult problems later.

14. We can transcend the script of a pre-defined story and pave the way for the future that we design. We just need to tap that power, that conviction, that determination within us. (Source – *Forbes*)

15. Not everyone wants to make the sacrifice in the trade-off to become wealthier, and the first part of that trade-off is savings and investment and time. (Source – Center Global Policy Solutions)

16. How do you spend your time?

17. The good news is, we follow people that look like us if the story is told the right way.

18. We've got these devices (the Internet) that you can tell a billion people your story in a matter of minutes.

19. You have the instinct to serve, and the skills to succeed. In fact, you have skills across a number of areas. Don't separate these skills; integrate them. The future will be written by those who integrate their whole being."

20. "African Americans, I think are some of the most interesting people on the planet. We've had some of the most challenging journeys, but we've brought so much joy. (Source – NMAAHC)

21. I am showing the current generations of African Americans they can do it, too. So the next generation can go even higher.

22. We have to do something for our community.

23. You should be able to drive to the airport and not be stopped three to seven times a year.

24. The single most important part of running and winning your own race is recognizing that you are enough and that you are an original.

25. I ran my own race. I knew what I wanted, and my persistence paid off,… (*Forbes*)

26. We are only bound by the limits of our own conviction.

27. I got hooked on technology,…..The excitement of figuring a complex problem out creates a eureka moment. It's one of the best moments in life.

28. With the process of discovery, you fail a lot,. And you learn a great deal from those failures, so the next time you can avoid those mistakes.

29. You can't be all things to everyone and still be effective.

30. I thought, 'If they could do it, so can I,…..Now I want people to say, 'If Robert Smith can do it, I can do that and more. (Source – *Washington Post*)

31. One of the things that inspired me earlier in my life was actually –believe it or not– the James Bond novels, because as I read them, they took me and transported me into places that I had no idea actually really existed.

Chapter 8

Success Rules from Bernard Arnault, Europe's Luxury Brand

Introduction to Billionaire Bernard Arnault – His Life and Contributions

Bernard Arnault, a name synonymous with luxury and success, is a French business magnate and the chairman and CEO of LVMH (Moët Hennessy Louis Vuitton), the world's leading luxury goods conglomerate. Born on March 5, 1949, in Roubaix, France, Arnault's journey from humble beginnings to becoming one of the wealthiest individuals on the planet is a testament to his unwavering ambition, entrepreneurial spirit, and relentless pursuit of excellence.

A renowned figure in the world of business and luxury, Arnault has left an indelible mark on the global industry. This biographical summary delves into the fascinating life and extraordinary achievements of Arnault, exploring his early life and background, his rise to success in business and entrepreneurship, and his significant contributions to the luxury industry. Additionally, we will examine the valuable lessons that can be gleaned from his career, delve into his philanthropic endeavors, and address the challenges and controversies he has faced. Finally, we will explore the lasting legacy and profound influence that Bernard Arnault has had on the business world as a whole.

1. Early Life and Background

1.1 Family and Cultural Influences

Bernard Arnault, the French business magnate and CEO of LVMH , was born into a family with a rich heritage in the construction industry. Growing up in the midst of this entrepreneurial environment, Arnault's family instilled in him the values of hard work, ambition, and determination. His upbringing played a significant role in shaping his mindset and laying the foundation for his future success.

1.2 Education and Early Career

Despite his family's involvement in construction, Arnault chose a different path by pursuing a degree in engineering and graduating from the prestigious École Polytechnique. Although this may seem like an unconventional choice for someone who would later become a luminary in the luxury industry, Arnault's engineering background provided him with a unique analytical approach to business.

After completing his education, Arnault joined his father's construction company, however, it wasn't long before he realized his true passion lay elsewhere. He had an innate entrepreneurial spirit and sought to explore new opportunities that aligned with his interests and ambitions. This led him to venture into the world of business and luxury, ultimately shaping his extraordinary career.

2. Rise to Success in Business and Entrepreneurship

2.1 Founding of Louis Vuitton Moët Hennessy (LVMH)

Arnault's most significant contribution to the business world came with the founding of LVMH in 1987. This multinational luxury goods conglomerate is now the leading player in the luxury sector, encompassing renowned brands such as Louis Vuitton, Dior, Fendi, and Givenchy.

2.2 Acquisitions and Expansion

Arnault's strategic vision and knack for recognizing lucrative opportunities fueled his relentless pursuit of acquisitions and expansion. Through a series of well-timed and astute acquisitions, he transformed LVMH into a global powerhouse. Notable acquisitions include the takeover of Louis Vuitton, the merger with Moët Hennessy, and the addition of prestigious brands like Bulgari and Tiffany & Co. to the LVMH portfolio.

2.3 Strategy and Leadership

Arnault's leadership style can be described as visionary and results-oriented. He strongly believes in empowering his teams and fostering a culture of creativity and innovation. Arnault's hands-on approach and attention to detail have been pivotal in maintaining LVMH's position as the epitome of luxury and excellence.

3. Contributions to the Luxury Industry

3.1 Revolutionizing the Fashion Industry

Arnault has played a significant role in revolutionizing the fashion industry. Under his guidance, LVMH's fashion brands have consistently pushed the boundaries of creativity, setting trends and shaping the global fashion landscape. His unwavering commitment to quality and craftsmanship has solidified LVMH's reputation as the pinnacle of luxury fashion.

3.2 Innovations in Marketing and Branding

Arnault's marketing genius has been instrumental in propelling luxury brands to unparalleled heights. His keen understanding of consumer behavior and evolving market trends has enabled LVMH to connect with a broader audience while maintaining an aura of exclusivity. The innovative marketing and branding strategies LVMH employs have become benchmarks for the industry as a whole.

3.3 Promoting Art and Culture

Beyond the world of fashion, Arnault recognizes the importance of art and culture. He has actively supported artistic endeavors, sponsoring exhibitions, and investing in prestigious art institutions. Arnault's commitment to nurturing the arts has not only enriched the cultural fabric of society, but also has positioned LVMH as a patron of creativity.

4. Lessons from Bernard Arnault's Career

4.1 Vision and Persistence

One of the key lessons to be learned from Bernard Arnault's career is the power of vision and persistence. Arnault's unwavering commitment to his goals, coupled with his ability to anticipate industry trends, has propelled him to the pinnacle of success. His vision and persistence serve as a reminder that pursuing one's dreams and standing firm in the face of challenges are crucial for achieving remarkable accomplishments.

4.2 Building and Nurturing Talent

Arnault's success is not solely attributable to his personal achievements, but also to his ability to identify and nurture talent. Throughout his career, he has surrounded himself with exceptional individuals who have played pivotal roles in driving LVMH's growth. This highlights the importance of building a strong team and empowering others to succeed.

4.3 Adapting to Market Trends

Arnault's career is a testament to the importance of adapting to market trends and staying ahead of the curve. He recognized the shifting dynamics within the luxury industry and seized opportunities to expand LVMH's portfolio accordingly. This ability to adapt has been instrumental in ensuring LVMH's continued success in an ever-evolving marketplace.

5. Philanthropic Endeavors and Social Impact

5.1 Commitment to Education and Youth Empowerment

Bernard Arnault understands that education is a key catalyst for social progress. He has shown his commitment to this cause by actively supporting various educational initiatives. Through the LVMH Group, he has established partnerships with universities and academic institutions to offer scholarships, internships, and training programs to young talents. By investing in education, Arnault aims to empower the next generation and provide them with the tools they need to succeed.

5.2 Environmental Sustainability Initiatives

In recognition of the pressing need for environmental conservation, Arnault has prioritized sustainability within his business ventures. The LVMH Group has implemented numerous sustainability practices, including reducing carbon emissions, optimizing energy efficiency, and promoting responsible sourcing. Arnault understands that luxury and environmental responsibility can go hand in hand, and he actively seeks to minimize the industry's ecological footprint.

5.3 Support for Health and Humanitarian Causes

Bernard Arnault is not only passionate about business, but he also deeply cares about the well-being of others. He has demonstrated this through his philanthropic efforts in supporting health and humanitarian causes. Arnault has made significant contributions to various organizations and foundations dedicated to improving healthcare, eradicating poverty, and providing aid during crises. His commitment to these causes highlights his belief in the importance of giving back and making a positive impact on society.

6. Arnault's Challenges and Controversies

6.1 Legal Battles and Corporate Governance Issues

Like any successful business figure, Bernard Arnault has faced his share of challenges and controversies. He has dealt with legal battles and corporate governance issues that have tested his leadership and strategic decision-making. Arnault's ability to navigate these challenges demonstrates his resilience and determination to protect his business interests while maintaining ethical standards.

6.2 Criticism and Public Perception

Being a prominent figure in the luxury industry, Arnault has also faced criticism and scrutiny from the public and media. Some have accused him of promoting excessive consumerism or being out of touch with the average person. Despite these criticisms, Arnault has remained focused on his goals, continuing to innovate and create luxury brands that resonate with consumers worldwide.

6.3 Balancing Business and Ethics

As a leader in the luxury industry, Arnault faces the challenge of balancing business objectives with ethical considerations. Operating in a sector often associated with opulence and extravagance, he strives to maintain a sense of responsibility and integrity. Arnault understands that sustainable business practices and ethical conduct are not only morally right, but also are crucial for long-term success and reputation.

7. Legacy and Influence in the Business World

7.1 Shaping the Luxury Industry Landscape

Bernard Arnault's contributions have left an indelible mark on the luxury industry. His visionary leadership and strategic acquisitions have shaped the landscape of luxury brands and brought them under the umbrella of the LVMH Group. His ability to identify and nurture talent has allowed iconic brands like Louis Vuitton, Fendi, and Dior to thrive and maintain their status as symbols of luxury and elegance.

7.2 Inspiring Future Entrepreneurs

Arnault's success story serves as an inspiration to aspiring entrepreneurs around the world. His journey from modest beginnings to becoming one of the richest individuals in the world demonstrates the power of ambition, perseverance, and strategic thinking. Arnault's entrepreneurial spirit encourages others to dream big and pursue their goals relentlessly, irrespective of their starting point.

7.3 Impact on Corporate Social Responsibility

Through his leadership and philanthropic endeavors, Bernard Arnault has had a significant impact on corporate social responsibility within the luxury industry and beyond. His emphasis on sustainability, education, and humanitarian causes sets an example for other businesses to follow. Arnault has shown that profitability and social responsibility can coexist, motivating other companies to integrate ethical practices into their operations and contribute positively to society.

In conclusion, Bernard Arnault's visionary approach, strategic mindset, and unwavering commitment to excellence have not only propelled him to great success, but also have reshaped the landscape of the luxury market. Moreover, his dedication to philanthropy and social causes highlights his deep understanding of the importance of giving back and making a positive impact on society. Bernard Arnault's legacy will continue to influence and inspire generations to come, leaving an enduring mark on the business world and beyond. Arnault's remarkable journey from humble beginnings to becoming a titan of the luxury industry serves as an inspiration to aspiring entrepreneurs and business leaders. His strategic acumen, relentless pursuit of excellence, and contributions to both business and culture have solidified his position as one of the most influential figures in the modern business landscape.

FAQs

1. What are some of Bernard Arnault's notable contributions to the luxury industry?

Bernard Arnault has made several significant contributions to the luxury industry. He is renowned for revolutionizing the fashion industry by introducing innovative marketing strategies, fostering collaborations with renowned designers, and acquiring prestigious fashion houses such as Dior, Givenchy, and Fendi. Arnault's visionary approach has transformed these brands into global icons of luxury and style.

2. How has Bernard Arnault made a difference through his philanthropic endeavors?

Bernard Arnault has demonstrated a strong commitment to philanthropy. Through his Foundation Louis Vuitton, he has supported various educational initiatives, including scholarships and programs aimed at fostering creativity and entrepreneurship among young people. Arnault also is dedicated to environmental sustainability, actively engaging in initiatives to reduce the carbon footprint and promote sustainable practices within the luxury industry.

3. What challenges and controversies has Bernard Arnault faced throughout his career?

Despite his immense success, Bernard Arnault has faced his fair share of challenges and controversies. He has been embroiled in legal battles and corporate governance issues, including conflicts over control of luxury conglomerate LVMH. Additionally, Arnault has faced criticism regarding his business practices, wealth accumulation, and perceived influence on the fashion industry. He has navigated these hurdles with resilience and continues to thrive in the global business arena.

4. What is Bernard Arnault's net worth?

His net worth is estimated at about $216 billion at the time of this writing.

Bernard Arnault's Success Rules, in His Own Words

- All that interests me is promoting my brands, never myself.

- Money is just a consequence. I always say to my team, don't worry too much about profitability.

- If you do your job well, the profitability will come.

- We don't like failures. We try to avoid them. That is why with many of our products, we make a limited number. We do not put the entire company at risk by introducing all new products all the time. In any given year, in fact, only 15% of our business comes from the new; the rest comes from traditional, proven products – the classics.

- I like that combination between creativity and the creative process and the organization needed to make a business like this successful worldwide.

- The goal of a startup is not to stay a startup. The goal of a startup is to grow and to become, if possible, a large company.

- Happiness for me is really leading the team and, if possible, leading them to the top.

- I take time to get close to, and I don't immediately throw my arms around someone.

- In business, I think the most important thing is to position yourself for long-term and not be too impatient.

- I am very competitive. I always want to win.

- If you control your distribution, you control your image.

- What feels good is choice. Having the freedom of choice.

- Luxury goods are the only area in which it is possible to make luxury margins.

- [On conducting a market test] You will never be able to predict the success of a product... Obviously we won't launch a product if the tests clearly show it is going to be a failure, but we won't use tests to modify products, either... Our strategy is to trust the creators. You have to give them leeway. When a creative team believes in a product, you have to trust the team's gut instinct.

- In the luxury business you have to build on heritage. On brands, on history... It's not an easy business, it's a business of passion that takes time. But when it's done right the potential is enormous.

- A star brand is current or you would call it fashionable. It is edgy, it has sex appeal, it is modern. In some way, it fulfils a fantasy. It is so new and unique; you want to buy it. You feel as if you must buy it, in fact, or else you won't be in the moment. You will be left behind.

- I like to see the reaction of the people in the shops. I also like to see the competition.

- I am quite competitive. I want to stay ahead and increase our advance.

- You need the right team of inspired managers.

On Creativity

- If you deeply appreciate and love what creative people do and how they think, which is usually in unpredictable and irrational ways, then you can start to understand them. And finally, you can see inside their minds and DNA.

- If you think and act like a typical manager around creative people — with rules, policies, data on customer preferences, and so forth — you will quickly kill their talent.

- It is not enough to have a talented designer; the management must be inspired too. The creative process is very disorganized; the production process has to be very rational.

- When something has to be done, do it! In France, we are full of good ideas, but we rarely put them into practice.

- If you look over a creative person's shoulder, he will stop doing great work. Wouldn't you, if some manager were watching your every move, clutching a calculator in his hand?

- Star brand is timeless, modern, fast growing, and highly profitable.

- I assure you, we do not lurk around every corner, questioning every creative decision. The most successful creative people... want to see their creations in the street. They don't invent just to invent.

- A new product is not creative — it is not important — if it does not shock when you first see it.

- They saw it was working. And then they said, 'Okay, now we are going to do the same thing.' I think, really, they underestimate the difficulty. They underestimate the time required to make it successful. And my guess is that they will have a very tough time.

- Working in the context of ultra-famous brands like Dior and Vuitton, creative spirits are always going to feel reined in. It's important that they are free to develop ideas. And rather than detracting from the principal job, it reinforces it. I think of that money as venture capital. It's not a big investment.

- The responsibility of the manager in a company dependent on innovation… becomes picking the right creative people — the ones who want to see their designs on the street.

Duplicate

- What made Louis Vuitton famous was the quality. We don't do marketing; we just create products which are exceptional in their design and craftsmanship.

- Products which are customer-driven are usually not innovative. Consequently, it is difficult to charge a premium.

- When you are on the management side, you still have to understand the artistic sensibility so that there is a dialogue with the creative side.

- [On philanthropy] It gives people working at the group a feeling that they don't exist only for cash flow, but for something bigger.

On Patience

- I think in business, you have to learn to be patient. Maybe I'm not very patient myself. But I think that I've learned the most is to be able to wait for something and get it when it's the right time.

- We are really very lucky to have so many fantastic brands. But to grow them we should not be too much in a hurry. They are growing fast, but they have to grow according to the market and to the capacity we have to deliver good products.

Chapter 9

TYLER PERRY'S SUCCES RULES

Introduction to Tyler Perry – His Life and Contributions

Tyler Perry is a name synonymous with success and inspiration in the business and film industry. From humble beginnings to becoming a renowned entrepreneur, filmmaker, and actor, Perry has carved a unique path to success, leaving an indelible mark on both the entertainment world and society at large. This article delves into the remarkable journey of Tyler Perry, exploring his early life, his significant contributions to the film industry, the valuable lessons that can be learned from his success, his philanthropic endeavors, and the enduring legacy he leaves behind. Join us as we unravel the fascinating story of Tyler Perry's life and the impact he has made.

1. Early Life and Background

1.1 Childhood and Family

Tyler Perry, the creative genius behind countless stage plays, movies, and television shows, was born on September 13, 1969, in New Orleans, Louisiana. Growing up in a challenging environment, Perry experienced poverty and abuse, which shaped his resilience and determination. Raised by his mother, Maxine, and with the support of his aunt, Tyler found solace in storytelling from an early age.

1.2 Early Career and Pursuit of Theatre

While his early life may not have been easy, Tyler Perry discovered his passion for entertainment as a means of escape. He began writing letters to himself as a form of therapy and self-expression, eventually translating these letters into plays. Perry faced numerous rejections and financial struggles before finally finding success with his play, *I Know I've Been Changed,* in 1992.

2. Journey into Business and Film Industry

2.1 Founding Tyler Perry Studios

In 2006, Tyler Perry made a bold move by founding Tyler Perry Studios in Atlanta, Georgia. This magnificent venture became the first major film studio owned by an African-American individual. With his determination and unwavering belief in his vision, Perry transformed a former army base into a 330-acre state-of-the-art facility that boasts 12 soundstages.

2.2 Breaking into Film and Television

Tyler Perry's remarkable journey extended beyond the stage to when he ventured into film and television. His popular character, Madea, a sharp-witted and sassy elderly woman played by Perry himself, became a beloved figure in several successful films. Additionally, Perry created and produced multiple television shows, including the hit drama series *The Haves and the Have Nots.*

3. Contributions to the Film Industry

3.1 Redefining African-American Representation

One of Tyler Perry's most significant contributions to the film industry is his commitment to showcasing diverse and authentic African-American characters and stories. Through his work, Perry has shattered stereotypes and introduced audiences to a multitude of narratives that highlight the rich diversity within the African-American community.

3.2 Box Office Success and Critical Acclaim

Tyler Perry's films have not only resonated with audiences, but also have achieved considerable financial success. Despite facing initial skepticism from Hollywood, Perry's movies consistently performed well at the box office, proving that there is a demand for stories that are often overlooked by mainstream studios. Moreover, Perry's talent has earned him numerous accolades, including several NAACP Image Awards and BET Honors.

4. Lessons from Tyler Perry's Success

4.1 Building a Brand and Staying True to Yourself

Tyler Perry's success can be attributed, in part, to his ability to build a brand that resonates with his audience. By staying true to his unique voice and creating content that speaks to his own experiences, Perry has cultivated a loyal fan base. This serves as a crucial reminder that authenticity is key when pursuing any creative endeavor.

4.2 Overcoming Challenges and Persistence

Tyler Perry's journey to success was not without its fair share of obstacles, but he never allowed them to deter him from his goals. Perry's determination, resilience, and the willingness to take risks played vital roles in his rise to fame. His story reminds us that with persistence and a belief in oneself, anything is possible.

Tyler Perry's impact on the entertainment industry is immense and a testament to the power of storytelling, perseverance, and authenticity. As he continues to create compelling content and give back to his community through philanthropy, Tyler Perry's influence will undoubtedly be felt for generations to come.

5. Philanthropic Endeavors and Social Impact

5.1 Supporting Causes and Giving Back

Tyler Perry is not only a successful entertainer and entrepreneur, but he also is known for his generous heart and passion for giving back to the community. Perry has been involved in various philanthropic endeavors over the years, supporting causes that are close to his heart. From donating to charities and organizations, to personally assisting families in need, Perry has made a significant impact on the lives of many.

One of the notable initiatives Perry has undertaken is his commitment to helping victims of natural disasters. In 2009, he provided temporary housing to hundreds of displaced families affected by Hurricane Katrina by offering up his own properties in Atlanta. Additionally, he has donated millions of dollars to organizations such as Feeding America, Covenant House, and the NAACP, among others.

5.2 Addressing Social Issues through Film and Television

Perry has also used his platform as a filmmaker to address social issues and spark important conversations. Through his work, he has tackled topics such as domestic violence, family dynamics, and the African American experience. His films and television shows often portray relatable characters and storylines that resonate with audiences, bringing attention to topics that may have been previously overlooked.

Perry's commitment to telling stories that matter has not gone unnoticed. He has been praised for his ability to shed light on important social issues while simultaneously entertaining audiences. By using his influence and creative talent, Perry has helped bring awareness to various societal challenges, and has become an advocate for positive change.

6. Tyler Perry's Entrepreneurial Ventures

6.1 Expansion into Various Business Ventures

Beyond his success in the entertainment industry, Perry has proven himself to be a savvy entrepreneur. He has expanded his brand into various business ventures, showcasing his versatility as a businessman. Perry has delved into the world of real estate, opening Tyler Perry Studios in Atlanta, one of the largest film studios in the United States. The studio has not only provided a space for his own productions but has also attracted other filmmakers and boosted the local economy.

In addition to his ventures in real estate, Perry has also ventured into other industries, including publishing. He has authored several books, sharing his personal journey and offering advice to aspiring entrepreneurs. Furthermore, Perry has launched his own production company, 34th Street Films, allowing him to extend his creative reach beyond his own projects.

6.2 The Tyler Perry Formula for Success

One of the keys to Perry's success as an entrepreneur is his unique formula. He has often shared his belief in the importance of taking risks, staying true to oneself, and embracing authenticity. Perry's distinctive voice and storytelling style have set him apart in the entertainment industry and have allowed him to build a dedicated fan base.

Moreover, Perry's business acumen is evident in his ability to recognize opportunities and adapt to changing market trends. He has showcased his versatility by creating content for both mainstream and niche audiences, ensuring that his work appeals to a wide range of viewers. By consistently delivering quality entertainment and staying ahead of the curve, Perry has solidified his position as a respected and influential figure in the business world.

7. Personal Life and Legacy of Tyler Perry

7.1 Balancing Personal and Professional Life

Despite his immense success, Tyler Perry has managed to maintain a balance between his personal and professional lives. He is known for being a private individual, keeping details about his personal life away from the spotlight. Perry also has spoken openly about the importance of family and the impact they have had on his journey.

Perry's personal life is centered around his son, Aman, whom he welcomed in 2014. Becoming a father has further inspired Perry to create content that speaks to families and highlights the importance of love, compassion, and forgiveness. He has shared that being a parent has brought a new level of joy and purpose to his life.

7.2 Tyler Perry's Enduring Legacy in the Entertainment Industry

Tyler Perry's enduring legacy in the entertainment industry cannot be overstated. Through his hard work, determination, and dedication to his craft, he has become a trailblazer and an inspiration to aspiring filmmakers and entrepreneurs alike. Perry's ability to connect with audiences through his relatable storytelling and his commitment to addressing important social issues has solidified his place in popular culture.

Moreover, Perry's philanthropic endeavors and his desire to give back have made a tangible impact on the lives of many. His generosity and support for various causes continue to make a difference in communities across the globe. Perry's legacy extends far beyond his success as an entertainer and entrepreneur; it is rooted in his commitment to uplifting others and using his platform for positive change.

In conclusion, Tyler Perry's biography is a testament to the power of determination, creativity, and philanthropy. From his early struggles to his groundbreaking success, Perry has not only transformed the film industry, but also has used his platform to address social issues and uplift others. His entrepreneurial ventures, lessons learned, and immense contributions have left an indelible mark on the entertainment world. As we reflect on his life and legacy, one thing is clear: Tyler Perry's influence will continue to inspire generations to come.

FAQs

1. How did Tyler Perry get started in the film industry?

Tyler Perry's journey into the film industry began with his stage plays that gained popularity in the 1990s. Recognizing the potential of his work, he took a leap of faith and self-funded his first feature film, *Diary of a Mad Black Woman*, which went on to achieve great success and launched his career in filmmaking.

2. What are some of Tyler Perry's most significant contributions to the film industry?

Tyler Perry's contributions to the film industry are multifaceted. He is known for creating a vast body of work that addresses important social issues, particularly within the African-American community. Perry has also played a significant role in promoting diversity and inclusivity in Hollywood and empowering underrepresented voices both in front of and behind the camera.

3. How has Tyler Perry used his success for philanthropic endeavors?

Tyler Perry has demonstrated a strong commitment to philanthropy throughout his career. He has donated generously to various charitable causes, including education, homelessness, and disaster relief. Perry has also used his resources to support aspiring artists and provide opportunities for individuals from disadvantaged backgrounds to pursue their dreams in the entertainment industry.

4. What is Tyler Perry's lasting legacy in the entertainment industry?

Tyler Perry's legacy in the entertainment industry extends beyond his immense success as a filmmaker and entrepreneur. He has become a trailblazer, breaking down barriers and paving the way for diverse storytelling. Perry's impact on representation and his ability to engage and resonate with diverse audiences have forever changed the landscape of film and television, leaving a lasting legacy for future African American generations.

5. What is Tyler Perry's net worth?

As at the time of writing, his net worth is estimated at about $1 billion.

Tyler Perry's Success Rules

Everything that happens to you can help you

1. Don't stop: Perry is known for both creating and performing as the Madea character, a tough elderly woman.

2. Challenge the thinking: He also creates films, some produced as live recordings of stage plays, and others professionally filmed using full sets and locations with full editing.

3. Own the show: He's estimated to have earned around $75 million by 2008.

4. Love working: Many of Perry's stage-play films have been subsequently adapted as professional films.

5. Know when to let go

6. Become your best self: He has also created several television shows, his most successful of which is Tyler Perry's House of Payne.

7. Never despise small beginnings: In 2012, Perry struck an exclusive multi-year partnership with Oprah Winfrey and her Oprah Winfrey Network.

8. Have fun: He has created multiple scripted series for the Oprah Winfrey Network, the most successful being *The Haves and the Have Nots*.

9. Be a student of life: As of 2014, *The Haves and the Have Nots* has given OWN its highest ratings to date.

10. Have faith.

11. Be a point of light: In his *Huffington Post* editorial, sociologist Shayne Lee lists Perry among the pantheon of today's most innovative filmmakers.

Tyler Perry Quotes on Owning your Dreams

- If you spread the water across many, many seeds, you don't have as much water for one seed.

- We don't have to wait for somebody to green light our projects, we can create our own intersections.

- Ideas are like wild horses in my head sometimes, and they're all over each other.

- All of the power that you have and all of the strength that you have and all the ideas that you have are in – or born in – your uniqueness.

- Focus on one thing, make it your priority and stick with it no matter what.

- Sometimes you have to be hidden, sometimes people are not supposed to recognize you.

- I'm a student of life and everyday something in my life is reminding me of something that I can write about.

- Everything that happens to you can work for your good if you let it.

- My only idea, my only focus was to do my one play, and I knew if could get that to work everything would come to pass.

- Focus on one thing, one area. Put all of your energy into watering one area.

Tyler Perry quotes on determination and reaching goals

- If you're trying to get there, you cannot stop believing.

- When something is for you, there is a feeling deep inside you that will not allow you to let it go.

- I wanna know why. Why is it done that way? Is there a better way to do it? Is there another way to do it?

- I'm not a rebel, but I've challenged the thinking.

- We don't have to be at the end of the line waiting for a handout, we can be at the front giving the hand up.

- "You can be born in a whole lot of a nightmare, but God can usher you into a dream."

- "I think it's very, very important that people have an opportunity to be the best of themselves."

- Never despise small beginnings.

- If you're struggling and you're fighting to be seen, sometimes you're supposed to be hidden…at the right time, God will reveal you, your talents, and everything you've done to the world.

- I like working with people who like to have fun because I don't think everything has to be serious.

Tyler Perry quotes to help you reach your highest potential

- I only wanna put out good things because I only want good things to come to me.

- All you can do is plant your seed in the ground, water it and believe. That's what allowed me to be in this position right now; I would not stop believing.

- Anything you want is possible, If I didn't believe it, I wouldn't take the time to send this message to you.

- When I built my studio, I built it in a neighborhood that's one of the poorest neighborhoods in Atlanta so that young black kids can see that a black man did that and they can do it too.

- The studio was once a Confederate Army base — and I want you to hear this — which meant that there were Confederate soldiers on that base, plotting and planning on how to keep 3.9 million Negroes enslaved. Now that land is owned by one Negro.

- Rather than being an icon, I wanna be an inspiration.

- Every dreamer in this room, there are people whose lives are tied to your dream. Own your stuff, own your business, own your way.

- When I started hiring Taraji, Viola Davis and Idris Elba, they couldn't get jobs in this town, but God blessed me to be in a position to be able to hire them. I was trying to help somebody cross.

- I want to own a network. I want to own a network where you can turn it on with your family all day long and get positive reinforcement.

- My biggest success is getting over the things that have tried to destroy and take me out of this life. Those are my biggest successes. It has nothing to do with work.

Tyler Perry quotes to inspire you to be stronger and live a better life

- While you're fighting for a seat at the table, I'll be down in Atlanta building my own. Because what I know for sure is that if I could just build this table, God will prepare it for me in the presence of my enemies.

- Be aware of the darkness, but your focus should always be the light.

- Share wisdom with those who will receive it.

- You give away your power when you don't forgive.

- I'm just enjoying my life. I suggest you try it.

- Don't let people change who you are, just be who you are with someone else.

- You can never be upset with the people who forced you into your dream.

- What I have learned in this life is, you can never be ashamed of where you come from.

- You can't make yourself happy by causing other people's misery.

- There will be rough nights but joy really does come in the morning.

Tyler Perry quotes to inspire and motivate you

- Fear is a spirit that really can stop you from living.

- Be careful what you say; life and death truly are in your own words.

- Are you living or just existing?

- People ask me all the time how did you make it? I say it in press all the time but people cut it out…it was nothing but the grace of God.

- It takes a while to build a dream.

- It doesn't matter if a million people tell you what you can't do, or if ten million people tell you no. If you get one yes from God, that's all you need.

- You can't build your life around hurts from the past.

- It's not an easy journey, to get to a place where you forgive people. But it is such a powerful place because it frees you.

- I don't think dreams die – I think that people give up.

- Stay in your lane and do what you're supposed to do.

More Tyler Perry quotes

- Once you're truly happy with yourself alone, that's when you are safe to find the right person to spend the rest of your life with.

- People always try to do the right thing…after they've tried everything else.

- We didn't have much, but we had love.

- A mother's love is stronger than distance, more powerful than time, and can transcend the grave.

- Don't try to be seen, God may be hiding you on purpose.

- What rings true is that everything we grow through in life will work out for our good.

- Being alone doesn't necessarily mean that you're lonely.

- The grass may be greener on the other side but the water bill is higher.

- You really will reap what you sew.

- God will really make your enemy your footstool.

- When it all comes down to it, life isn't about how much we get - it's about how much we share.

- You let your past destroy you, or you use it to create something better

- Once you're truly happy with yourself alone, that's when you are safe to find the right person to spend the rest of your life with.

- Rather than focus on your critics, focus on the people who are impacted by your work.

- Don't wait for someone to green light your project, build your own intersection.

- If I'm away from you for more than an hour, I can't stop thinking about you. I carry you in my spirit. I pray for you more than I pray for myself...I know you don't believe in fairy tales. But, if you did, I'd want to be your knight in shining armor. You've been through so much. I don't want to see you hurt anymore. Now I may not be able to give you all that you're used to. But I do know I can love you past your pain. I don't want you to worry about anything. You just wake up in the morning, that's all you have to do and I'll take it from there...There's one condition...You have to be my wife.

- I always feed myself positivity. I turn to anything that teaches good, that teaches strength, and that you can make it. I swear to you that those kinds of thoughts come alive in your body and in anything you touch because your energy goes into everything you touch, everything you share and everything you speak. So, it's most important that you surround yourself with positivity always and have it in your mind at all times.

- Focus on one thing; make it your priority, and stick with it no matter what!

- The key to life when it gets tough is to keep moving. Just keep moving.

- You know, people don't want their intelligence insulted. They don't want to be preached to. They don't want to be degraded. All they want to do is sit, laugh, have a good time, love one another, forget about what's going on in the world, and find something out so they can be useful in this life. Do this and you have common sense.

- The road that I'm on is a path that I didn't choose. It chose me. I'm just trying to walk it, and to do the best that I can to honor and respect it.

- Fear is a sprit that really can stop you from living.

- A mother's love is stronger than distance, more powerful than time and can transcend the grave.

- I live my life outside of the box because when I die they're going to put me into one!

- When you haven't forgiven those who've hurt you, you turn back against your future. When you do forgive, you start walking forward.

- God has put me in a really good position where I can make the choices to walk away if something is not right, so that way I can keep my integrity.

- It's not an easy journey, to get to a place where you forgive people. But it is such a powerful place because it frees you.

- You can get a thousand no's from people, and only one "yes" from God.

- You can get a thousand no's from people, and only one "yes" from God.

Sources: AZ Quotes, https://www.azquotes.com/author/11559-Tyler_Perry June 27, 2021.

Everyday Power, https://everydaypower.com/tyler-perry-quotes/ June 27, 2021.

BILL GATES' SUCCESS RULES

Introduction to Bill Gates – His Life and Contributions

Gates was born and raised in Seattle, Washington. In 1975, he and Paul Allen founded Microsoft in Albuquerque, New Mexico. It became the world's largest personal computer software company. Gates led the company as chairman and CEO until stepping down as CEO in January 2000, succeeded by Steve Ballmer, but he remained chairman of the board of directors and became chief software architect. Bill Gates is one of the most influential figures in the tech industry, as well as a prominent philanthropist. This biographical summary delves into Gates' remarkable journey, exploring his early life and education; the founding of Microsoft; his contributions to the tech industry; his philanthropic efforts, and the valuable lessons that can be learned from his life and career. Through an examination of his achievements and impact, we gain insights into the mind of a visionary entrepreneur and a committed humanitarian.

1. Early Life and Education

1.1 Childhood and Family Background

Bill Gates, born on October 28, 1955, in Seattle, Washington, had a childhood that was far from ordinary. Growing up in a family that valued education and entrepreneurship, he was exposed to the world of business at a young age. His father, William H. Gates, Sr., was a prominent lawyer, and his mother, Mary Maxwell Gates, served on corporate boards. This environment of ambition and intellectual curiosity laid the foundation for Gates' future success.

1.2 Education and Academic Achievements

Gates attended the prestigious Lakeside School, where he first discovered his passion for computers. He became engrossed in programming and showed remarkable aptitude in the field. Recognizing his talent, Lakeside administrators allowed him to have unlimited access to a mainframe computer, a luxury few could afford at the time. This access helped Gates develop his programming skills and ignited his entrepreneurial spirit. Later, Gates enrolled at Harvard University but decided to drop out to pursue his business endeavors full-time. Despite leaving college, his determination and intellect would ultimately propel him to great heights.

2. Founding of Microsoft and Business Success

2.1 Inspiration and Early Entrepreneurial Ventures

Before the founding of Microsoft, Gates and his childhood friend, Paul Allen, collaborated on various ventures. In 1975, they co-founded Microsoft, then known as Micro-Soft, with the vision of putting a computer on every desk and in every home. Their early projects included developing programming languages and creating software for microcomputers, which laid the groundwork for their future success.

2.2 Founding of Microsoft and Evolution of the Company

The official establishment of Microsoft marked the beginning of its evolution into a global technology powerhouse. Gates played a pivotal role in shaping the company's culture and strategic direction. Under his leadership, Microsoft pioneered the operating system MS-DOS, which became the foundation for its subsequent successes. The company then expanded into developing user-friendly software such as Windows, Office, and Internet Explorer, dominating the personal computer industry.

2.3 Key Business Strategies and Milestones

Gates' business genius was evident in the key strategies he employed to solidify Microsoft's position in the market. He embraced partnerships, forging alliances with IBM and other tech giants to ensure wider adoption of Microsoft's software. Additionally, Gates recognized the importance of acquiring innovative companies and technologies, leading Microsoft to acquire significant players like Skype, LinkedIn, and GitHub. These strategic moves cemented Microsoft's dominance and propelled its growth trajectory.

3. Contributions to the Tech Industry

3.1 Development and Advancements in Software

Gates' contributions to the tech industry are best exemplified by his relentless focus on software development and innovation. With a keen eye for identifying market needs, he led Microsoft in creating groundbreaking products like the Windows operating system, which revolutionized personal computing. The company's software advancements have since played a crucial role in shaping modern technology and empowering individuals and businesses worldwide.

3.2 Impact and Influence on Personal Computing

Gates' vision of a computer for every individual was realized through his relentless advocacy for personal computing. By making technology more accessible and intuitive, he transformed computers from esoteric machines into indispensable tools for everyday life. Microsoft's software, particularly Windows, played a vital role in this evolution by providing a user-friendly interface that opened doors for millions of people to embrace the digital age.

3.3 Innovation in Internet Technologies

Recognizing the immense potential of the internet, Gates led Microsoft's foray into the online world. Internet Explorer, Microsoft's web browser, became a key driver in popularizing internet usage and making it more accessible to a wider audience. This innovation laid the groundwork for the internet revolution we experience today, connecting people, businesses, and knowledge on a global scale.

4. Philanthropic Efforts and the Bill & Melinda Gates Foundation

4.1 Establishment and Objectives of the Gates Foundation

Bill Gates' philanthropic journey began in 1994 with the establishment of the William H. Gates Foundation, later renamed the Bill & Melinda Gates Foundation. The foundation's primary objectives are to enhance healthcare, reduce poverty, and expand educational opportunities across the globe. With a focus on tackling complex issues, the Gates Foundation aims to create lasting change and improve the quality of life for people around the world.

4.2 Areas of Philanthropic Focus and Initiatives

The Gates Foundation has made significant contributions in various areas, including global health, education, and agricultural development. Through partnerships and collaborative efforts, it has played a crucial role in eradicating diseases like polio and malaria, improving healthcare infrastructure, and advancing educational opportunities for underprivileged communities. The foundation's initiatives also address issues such as gender equality, clean energy, and economic development, reflecting Gates' commitment to tackling multifaceted challenges.

4.3 Global Impact and Collaborative Partnerships

Gates' philanthropy has had a remarkable global impact. By leveraging his wealth and influence, he has ignited a spirit of giving among billionaires through initiatives like the Giving Pledge, which encourages the wealthy to commit the majority of their wealth to charitable causes. Collaborative partnerships with governments, academic institutions, and other organizations have allowed the Gates Foundation to amplify its impact and create sustainable change on a large scale. Through his philanthropic efforts, Gates continues to inspire others to use their resources for the betterment of humanity.

5. Lessons Learned from Bill Gates's Life and Career

5.1 Entrepreneurial and Leadership Insights

If there's one thing we can learn from Bill Gates, it's that being an entrepreneur isn't just about having a great idea; it's about having the passion, drive, and determination to turn that idea into reality. Gates co-founded Microsoft with a vision to put a computer on every desk and in every home, and he never wavered from that goal. His relentless pursuit of innovation, combined with his ability to lead and inspire a team, allowed Microsoft to become one of the most successful companies in the world.

5.2 The Importance of Persistence and Adaptability

Bill Gates's journey to success was not without its challenges. From facing legal battles to competing against giants in the industry, Gates encountered numerous obstacles along the way, but he never gave up. His persistence and ability to adapt to changing circumstances were instrumental in overcoming these hurdles. Whether it was navigating the rapidly evolving tech landscape or responding to market demands, Gates showed that being open to change and staying resilient are essential qualities for achieving long-term success.

5.3 Balancing Business Success with Social Responsibility

While Gates undoubtedly revolutionized the computer industry, he didn't stop there. Through his philanthropic efforts, he has dedicated himself to improving the lives of people around the world. The Bill and Melinda Gates Foundation, established by Gates and his wife, has made significant contributions in areas such as healthcare, education, and poverty alleviation. Gates's commitment to giving back serves as a reminder that success should not only be measured by financial achievements but also by the impact we have on others.

Bill Gates's life and career offer invaluable lessons for aspiring entrepreneurs and leaders. From his entrepreneurial and leadership insights to his emphasis on persistence, adaptability, and social responsibility, Gates's journey serves as an inspiration for those who seek to make a difference. So let's take a page out of Gates's book, embrace our passions, overcome challenges with resilience, and remember to give back along the way. After all, as Gates himself once said, "To win big, you sometimes have to take big risks."

In conclusion, Bill Gates's biography reveals a life filled with groundbreaking achievements in the tech industry and a deep commitment to making a positive impact on the world. From the founding of Microsoft to his philanthropic efforts through the Bill & Melinda Gates Foundation, Gates has left an indelible mark on both business and society. His journey serves as an inspiration for aspiring entrepreneurs, emphasizing the importance of innovation, perseverance, and the responsibility to give back. As we reflect on Gates's life and career, we are reminded of the power of combining success with philanthropy, creating a lasting legacy that extends far beyond business accomplishments.

FAQs

1. What are some of Bill Gates's notable contributions to the tech industry?

Bill Gates has made several notable contributions to the tech industry. He co-founded Microsoft, which revolutionized personal computing with the development of the Windows operating system. Gates also played a pivotal role in the advancement of software and Internet technologies, shaping the way we interact with computers and the online world.

2. How has Bill Gates's philanthropy made a difference?

Bill Gates's philanthropy has made a significant difference in various areas. Through the Bill & Melinda Gates Foundation, he has focused on improving global health, addressing poverty, and enhancing education. The foundation's initiatives have led to advancements in vaccination programs, access to quality healthcare, poverty alleviation efforts, and educational opportunities for underprivileged communities.

3. What lessons can we learn from Bill Gates's life and career?

Bill Gates's life and career offer valuable lessons for aspiring entrepreneurs and individuals interested in making a positive impact. Some key lessons include the importance of perseverance, adaptability, and continuous learning. Gates's success also highlights the significance of combining business achievements with social responsibility, demonstrating the transformative power of using wealth and influence to address pressing global issues.

4. What is Bill Gates' Net worth?

Bill Gates net worth is currently estimated at $114.4 billion at the time of this writing.

Bill Gates' Success Rules, in His Own Words

1. Start as Early as Possible

Bill Gates was only 13 years old when he started working with computers. When you start something at an early point in your life, you become molded around it. Not only will you have a chance of becoming successful sooner than most people, but you would also be less likely to want to give up. If you've had a dream that you start working towards when you're young, you will be more immune to people telling you what you can or can't do. By the time you're an adult and people actually start to take more notice of what you're working towards, you will be stubborn enough to just ignore them.

The time that you're most influenced by others is when you're younger, so if you've seen things on TV or on the Internet where others have become successful, this will be imprinted in your mind and you won't have doubt about what you can or can't do.

2. Enter into Partnerships

Bill Gates was very fond of forming partnerships with people, people who were the top dog and that made Gates become the 'sidekick'. He was happy with this because it unlocked new opportunities for him and the potential to learn from other successful entrepreneurs who could teach him a thing or two. Not only that, but it meant that he built relationships with people that would definitely be able to help him out with his future endeavors.

3. You Will Not Make $60,000 a Year Right out of High School

Let's be honest, you're not going to make $60,000 a year straight out of high school, so if for some reason you think you will, stop kidding yourself. No matter how much education you have, you still need the experience to work your way to the top. You won't get appointed CEO of a multi-national company just because you have a degree in business management. That's a position that you need to earn, by either starting your own company and working hard to take it to the top or working your way up within a company and proving yourself to people.

4. Be Your Own Boss as Soon as Possible

Bill Gates became a boss at a fairly early age. He deserved it, and it put him in an excellent position with pure control over his success.

5. Don't Whine About Your Mistakes, Learn from Them

What is the point in blaming other people for your mistakes? Who are you trying to fool? Your mistakes are on you, they are not anyone else's fault, so stop blaming other people just to try and rid your conscience of guilt. Mistakes are made to be learned from. You now know what or what not to do in the same situation when it rolls around for a second time and, believe me, in most cases it will roll around again.

6. Be Committed and Passionate

I think this is always included by every entrepreneur as a good bit of advice. You need to be committed to what you love and have a great passion for what you do. The successful people in this world make it look so easy because they absolutely love what they are doing. If you're finding things too stressful and too hard, then I'm not sure you're working on the right thing.

7. Life is the Best School, Not University or College

No matter how many books you read, no matter how many tests you take, nothing from university or college can properly prepare you for life in the real world. Real-life jobs and bosses do not just involve you studying and them teaching you. It's real-life work that you need to be able to carry out, otherwise, you will be fired. End of story.

8. Be Nice to Nerds

It's true, people who you'd probably class as nerds are actually the ones who will work the hardest, be the smartest, and be determined to succeed. If you're horrible to nerds then you're basically taking your chances with fate because you could easily end up working for one, or even apply for a position at a company that is run by someone you know and have been horrible to in the past.

9. TV is Not Real Life

You need to stop getting sucked into television and believing that what you're seeing in some cases may actually be what people do in real life. Real-life is tough and anybody who's anywhere near successful will not be sitting around in coffee shops all day talking to their friends. They will be out working the grind to pay their bills and improve their financial situation.

10. Life is Not Fair

Another of Bill Gates' success lessons is to learn that life is not fair. No matter how hard you work in life, there will always be times where things don't go your way, perhaps through no fault of your own. Things that you cannot control. You will get knocked down, but you need to be able to stand up. Life isn't fair. It's a test, a game, a risk. If you fall down and don't bother getting back up, you don't deserve to be successful. Winners know that life isn't fair and they will keep getting back up until they've made it.

11. Be Ready to Takes Risks

Starting a business is a little bit like gambling; you're not always sure if you'll win or not. The only difference is that you can strategize and plan well enough to ensure the success of your business.

12. Never Fast Forward Your Way to Success

Nothing comes easy and that includes being successful. Bill Gates and Paul Allen started Microsoft on a shaky foundation, but through patience and hard work, they were able to surpass the struggles they encountered. This just goes to show that there are no shortcuts to success, my friend. It takes time to build an empire and a lifetime of sacrifice to keep the consistency going.

13. Be Proud of Who You Are

Many people get frustrated because they're not as smart, rich or talented as the person they look up to. You may get frustrated because you're not as successful as Bill Gates, but you have to face the reality that we're all born differently. Each person has their own unique abilities, and to become successful you have to accept that. If you start to appreciate yourself and what you can offer, you will be more confident to do things your own way.

14. Be Humble at All Times

It's great to dream of success and all that comes with it. However, if you let it get into your head and start to think that you're untouchable, that is not what you call success.

Life is a wheel, it's unpredictable. You can be on top today but at the bottom the next. (Trust me!) It's best to stay humble at all times and never forget what got you there in the first place.

15. Take Things Positively & Love Learning

Bill Gates also had his fair share of unsatisfied customers, but he never considered this as something negative. Instead, he took their insights to heart and used them to improve his work.

When people hear criticism and bad feedback, they are easily discouraged and their drive to succeed goes downhill. But if you think about it, this negativity will help you more than you realize, if you look closely. Learn from your mistakes and shortcomings and use that as a catalyst to be the best in what you do.

16. Accept Failures and Move On

Failures are more important than success, because by failing you become successful. The greatest life lessons and the knowledge that changes everything – are found when you fail.

When you succeed, you can learn lessons, you are happy, people will praise you and everyone is willing to help you. But when you fail, everything is dark and you'll know how it is to suffer. You will see the real ones from the fake ones. More than the joy that success brings you, always place greater importance on the lessons you learned when you failed. Use that as your weapon as you go through life's journey.

17. Share Your Success With Others

You know the feeling of being an owner of a small startup. It's difficult and you have probably experienced many struggles. A truly successful entrepreneur will support and share his or her knowledge with other aspiring entrepreneurs, giving them the encouragement and inspiration they need.

Bill Gates Quotes About What Successful People Do

- Be nice to nerds. Chances are you'll end up working for one.

- It's fine to celebrate success, but it is more important to heed the lessons of failure.

- Success is a lousy teacher. It seduces smart people into thinking they can't lose.

- Television is not real life. In real life, people actually have to leave the coffee shop and go to jobs.

- We always overestimate the change that will occur in the next two years and underestimate the change that will occur in the next ten. Don't let yourself be lulled into inaction.

- Life is not divided into semesters. You don't get summers off, and very few employers are interested in helping you. Find yourself.

- Before you were born, your parents weren't as boring as they are now. They got that way from paying your bills, cleaning your clothes, and listening to you talk about how cool you thought you were. So before you save the rain forest from the parasites of your parents' generation, try delousing the closet in your own room.

- I'm a big believer that as much as possible, and there's obviously political limitations, freedom of migration is a good thing.

- Of my mental cycles, I devote maybe 10% to business thinking. Business isn't that complicated.

Bill Gates Quotes That Will Inspire you to Change the World

- I believe that if you show people the problems and you show them the solutions they will be moved to act.

- Technology is just a tool. In terms of getting the kids working together and motivating them, the teacher is the most important.

- Your most unhappy customers are your greatest source of learning.

- We all need people who will give us feedback. That's how we improve.

- I'm a great believer that any tool that enhances communication has profound effects in terms of how people can learn from each other, and how they can achieve the kind of freedoms that they're interested in.

- As we look ahead into the next century, leaders will be those who empower others.

- If GM had kept up with technology like the computer industry has, we would all be driving $25 cars that got 1,000 MPG.

- I believe in innovation and that the way you get innovation is you fund research and you learn the basic facts.

- Everyone needs a coach. It doesn't matter whether you're a basketball player, a tennis player, a gymnast or a bridge player.

- I really had a lot of dreams when I was a kid, and I think a great deal of that grew out of the fact that I had a chance to read a lot.

Bill Gates Quotes to Enrich your Life

- Expectations are a form of first-class truth: If people believe it, it's true.

- The general idea of the rich helping the poor, I think, is important.

- This is a fantastic time to be entering the business world, because business is going to change more in the next 10 years than it has in the last 50.

- Our success has really been based on partnerships from the very beginning.

- If you can't make it good, at least make it look good.

- Until we're educating every kid in a fantastic way, until ever inner city is cleaned up, there is no shortage of things to do.

- If you think your teacher is tough, wait until you get a boss. He doesn't have tenure.

- If I'd had some set idea of a finish line, don't you think I would have crossed it years ago?

- We've got to put a lot of money into changing behavior.

- I do think this next century, hopefully, will be about a more global view. Where you don't just think, 'Yes, my country is doing well,' but you think about the world at large.

Bill Gates Quotes on Leadership

- There is a certain responsibility that accrued to me when I got to this unexpected position.

- You see, antiquated ideas of kindness and generosity are simply bugs that must be programmed out of our world. And these cold, unfeeling machines show us the way.

- The most amazing philanthropists are people who are actually making a significant sacrifice.

- I have been struck again and again by how important measurement is to improving the human condition.

- I was lucky to be involved and get to contribute to something that was important, which is empowering people with software.

- I believe the returns on investment in the poor are just as exciting as successes achieved in the business arena, and they are even more meaningful!

- Whether I'm at the office, at home, or on the road, I always have a stack of books I'm looking forward to reading.

- Who decides what's in Windows? The customers who buy it.

- The best teacher is very interactive.

- In business, the idea of measuring what you are doing, picking the measurements that count like customer satisfaction and performance… you thrive on that.

Bill Gates Quotes on Success

- Effective philanthropy requires a lot of time and creativity – the same kind of focus and skills that building a business requires.

- We make the future sustainable when we invest in the poor, not when we insist on their suffering.

- Americans want students to get the best education possible. We want schools to prepare children to become good citizens and members of a prosperous American economy.

- The way to be successful in the software world is to come up with breakthrough software, and so whether it's Microsoft Office or Windows, its pushing that forward. New ideas, surprising the marketplace, so good engineering and good business are one in the same.

- To win big, you sometimes have to take big risks.

- Don't compare yourself with anyone in this world. If you do so, you are insulting yourself.

- The best way to prepare [to be a programmer] is to write programs, and to study great programs that other people have written. In my case, I went to the garbage cans at the Computer Science Center and fished out listings of their operating system.

- I studied everything but never stopped. But today the toppers of the best universities are my employees

- In this business, by the time you realize you are in trouble, it's too late to save yourself. Unless you're running scared all the time, you're gone.

- In my view, investing in public libraries is an investment in the nation's future.

Motivational Bill Gates Quotes and Sayings

- Business is a money game with few rules and a lot of risk.

- Innovation is moving at a scarily fast pace. The vision is about empowering workers, giving them all the information about what's going on so they can do a lot more than they've done in the past."

- Life is not fair, get used to it.

- I choose a lazy person to do a hard job. Because a lazy person will find an easy way to do it.

- A bad strategy will fail no matter how good your information is, and lame execution will stymie a good strategy. If you do enough things poorly, you will go out of business.

- If you are born poor it's not your mistake, But if you die poor it's your mistake.

- A fundamental new rule for business is that the Internet changes everything.

- Money has no utility to me beyond a certain point.

- I am not in competition with anyone but myself. My goal is to improve myself continuously.

More Bill Gates Quotes

- If you give people tools, and they use their natural abilities and their curiosity, they will develop things in ways that will surprise you very much beyond what you might have expected.

- Measuring programming progress by lines of code is like measuring aircraft building progress by weight.

- Power comes not from knowledge kept but from knowledge shared.

- In particular, green premiums are a fantastic lens for making decisions.

- It wasn't enough to deliver cheap, reliable energy for the poor. It also had to be clean.

Source: Everyday Power, https://everydaypower.com/bill-gates-quotes/. June 28, 2021. All rights reserved.

Chapter 11

Success Rules of Carlos Slim Helu, Mexico's Richest Billionaire

Introduction to Carlos Slim Helu: His Life and Contributions

Carlos Slim Helu, a Mexican business magnate and philanthropist, is widely recognized as one of the most influential and successful entrepreneurs of our time. Born on January 28, 1940, in Mexico City, Slim's journey from a modest upbringing to amassing a vast empire of businesses and investments is nothing short of remarkable. This article delves into the biography, life, business ventures, philanthropy, and lessons learned from Carlos Slim Helu, shedding light on his extraordinary contributions to various industries and his profound impact on society.

1. Background and Early Life

1.1 Childhood and Family Background

Carlos Slim Helu, born on January 28, 1940, in Mexico City, comes from a modest background. His parents, Julian Slim Haddad and Linda Helu Atta, were Lebanese immigrants who instilled in Carlos the values of hard work and perseverance. Growing up in a large family, Carlos developed an understanding of the importance of unity and collaboration.

1.2 Education and Influences

Education played a crucial role in shaping Carlos Slim's future. He attended the National Autonomous University of Mexico (UNAM), where he obtained a degree in civil engineering. This background in engineering gave him a unique perspective, allowing him to approach business challenges with a problem-solving mindset.

Carlos Slim was also greatly influenced by his father, who was a successful businessman himself. His father's emphasis on the importance of investing in assets and maintaining strong financial discipline left a lasting impact on Carlos's approach to business.

2. Building an Empire: Carlos Slim's Business Ventures and Successes

2.1 Early Business Ventures and Investments

Carlos Slim's entrepreneurial journey began early on. While still in college, he started buying shares in Mexican companies, eventually amassing a significant portfolio. Slim's sharp business acumen and ability to identify undervalued assets allowed him to make smart investments that yielded substantial returns.

2.2 Acquisitions and Expansion

As his wealth grew, Carlos Slim continued to expand his business empire. He acquired numerous companies across diverse sectors, including telecommunications, finance, construction, and retail. Notable acquisitions include Telmex, the largest telecommunications company in Mexico, and Grupo Carso, which encompasses a wide range of industries.

2.3 Diversification and Key Holdings

Carlos Slim's success can be attributed, in part, to his strategy of diversification. By holding significant stakes in various industries, he ensured a balanced investment portfolio. Some of his key holdings include America Movil, one of the largest mobile network operators in the world, and Grupo Financiero Inbursa, a leading financial services company in Mexico.

3. The Carlos Slim Foundation: Philanthropy and Social Contributions

3.1 Foundation's Mission and Initiatives

Carlos Slim's philanthropic endeavors are as impressive as his business achievements. The Carlos Slim Foundation, established in 1986, aims to improve the quality of life for people in Mexico and beyond. The foundation focuses on education, healthcare, and sustainable development, addressing some of the most pressing societal issues.

3.2 Impact on Education and Healthcare

Through various initiatives, the Carlos Slim Foundation has made significant contributions to education and healthcare. It has provided scholarships, built schools and educational centers, and supported research in various fields. Additionally, the foundation has funded numerous healthcare programs, aiming to enhance access to medical services and improve public health.

3.3 Collaborations and Partnerships

Recognizing the need for collaboration to achieve lasting change, the Carlos Slim Foundation actively collaborates with governments, NGOs, and other organizations. By leveraging partnerships, the foundation maximizes its impact and implements sustainable solutions. It serves as a catalyst for positive change, inspiring others to join efforts in creating a better future.

4. Life Lessons from Carlos Slim: Insights into Success and Leadership

4.1 Principles and Values that Shaped Carlos Slim's Approach

Carlos Slim's success can be attributed to several principles and values he holds dear. He believes in long-term thinking, patient capital, and maintaining financial discipline. Carlos emphasizes the importance of continuous learning, adaptability, and embracing technological advancements to stay ahead in a rapidly changing world.

4.2 Strategies for Business Success

One of Carlos Slim's key strategies for business success is identifying undervalued assets and seizing opportunities when others hesitate. He also stresses the significance of building strong teams, fostering a culture of innovation, and focusing on customer satisfaction. By prioritizing efficiency and cost-effectiveness, Slim has been able to achieve sustainable growth and profitability.

4.3 Leadership Lessons and Management Style

Carlos Slim's leadership style is characterized by his hands-on approach and attention to detail. He values teamwork, encourages open communication, and delegates responsibilities effectively. Slim believes in leading by example and nurturing talent within his organizations. His humility and commitment to giving back to society have earned him respect both as a businessman and a leader.

5. Carlos Slim's Influence on the Global Economy and Industries

5.1 Impact on Telecommunications Sector

Carlos Slim Helu, the Mexican business magnate, has left an indelible mark on the global economy and various industries. In the telecommunications sector, Slim's influence has been nothing short of revolutionary. Through his telecommunications company, Telmex, he has played a pivotal role in connecting people across Mexico and beyond. Whether it's landlines or mobile networks, Slim's vision and investments have transformed the way we communicate. Love it or hate it, you can't deny the impact of Slim's telecom empire.

5.2 Contributions to the Retail Industry

Slim's entrepreneurial prowess extends beyond telecommunications. His contributions to the retail industry are equally noteworthy. With his retail conglomerate, Grupo Sanborns, Slim has managed to shape the shopping experience for millions. From bookstores to department stores, his business ventures have become household names in Mexico. And let's not forget his involvement in the global giant, Walmart. Slim's influence in the retail sector is a testament to his shrewd business acumen and ability to adapt to changing consumer demands.

5.3 Influence on Infrastructure Development

When it comes to infrastructure development, Carlos Slim's fingerprints can be found all over the world. His company, Grupo Carso, has been instrumental in building and improving crucial infrastructure projects. From highways and bridges to energy plants and real estate, Slim's influence extends far beyond the realm of telecommunications and retail. His commitment to investing in infrastructure has not only boosted economic growth but has also contributed to job creation and improved living standards.

6. Challenges and Criticisms: Examining Controversies Surrounding Carlos Slim

6.1 Monopoly Allegations and Anti-Competitive Practices

With great power comes great scrutiny, and Carlos Slim has faced his fair share of controversies. One of the most significant criticisms leveled against him is the allegation of creating monopolies and engaging in anti-competitive practices. Critics argue that Slim's dominance in certain industries has stifled competition and limited consumer choice. While it's essential to acknowledge his achievements, it's equally crucial to address the valid concerns surrounding fair market practices.

6.2 Criticisms of Wealth Accumulation and Income Inequality

Another aspect that has drawn criticism is the accumulation of vast wealth by Slim and its impact on income inequality. As one of the richest individuals in the world, Slim's fortune has raised questions about wealth distribution and economic disparity. While he has undoubtedly made significant contributions to society, critics argue that more should be done to address income inequality and ensure a fair distribution of resources. These concerns highlight the ongoing debate about the responsibilities of the super-wealthy in narrowing the wealth gap.

6.3 Responding to Public Scrutiny and Legal Battles

Public scrutiny and legal battles have become a part of Carlos Slim's life as he navigates through his business empire. From government investigations to labor disputes, he has faced numerous challenges over the years. However, his ability to weather these storms and continue making significant contributions is a testament to his resilience. Though controversies and legal battles have marred his reputation, they haven't detracted from his achievements or his influence on various industries.

7. Legacy and Impact: Carlos Slim's Enduring Contributions to Society

7.1 Long-Term Economic and Social Impact

Regardless of controversies and criticisms, Carlos Slim's contributions to society have left an undeniably lasting impact. His investments in industries like telecommunications and retail have created jobs, stimulated economic growth, and shaped the way we live and interact.

The long-term economic and social impact of his ventures cannot be underestimated.

7.2 Philanthropic Legacy and Continued Influence

Beyond business, Carlos Slim's philanthropic endeavors have also left a significant mark. Through his charitable foundation, Fundación Carlos Slim, he has supported initiatives in education, healthcare, and cultural preservation. From funding scholarships to improving access to healthcare in underserved communities, Slim's philanthropy showcases a commitment to making a positive difference in society. Even as he continues to shape industries, his philanthropic legacy is a reminder that wealth can be used for the greater good.

8. Reflecting on Carlos Slim's Life and Contributions

Carlos Slim Helu's life and contributions are a reflection of his unparalleled business acumen, entrepreneurial spirit, and commitment to improving society. While controversies and criticisms have surrounded his success, it is essential to recognize the undeniable impact he has had on the global economy, industries, and philanthropy. Carlos Slim's story serves as a reminder that success comes with responsibility and the power to make a difference in the lives of others.

Carlos Slim Helu's journey from a modest background to becoming one of the wealthiest individuals in the world is nothing short of remarkable. His business acumen, philanthropy, and leadership serve as an inspiration for aspiring entrepreneurs and leaders worldwide.

FAQs

1. What are Carlos Slim Helu's most notable business ventures?

Carlos Slim Helu is known for his involvement in a wide range of industries. Some of his most notable business ventures include telecommunications companies such as Telmex and América Móvil, retail conglomerate Grupo Sanborns, infrastructure development projects, and investments in banking and finance sectors.

2. How has Carlos Slim contributed to philanthropy?

Carlos Slim Helu is a dedicated philanthropist who has made significant contributions through the Carlos Slim Foundation. His foundation focuses on various initiatives, including education, healthcare, and sustainable development. Slim's philanthropic efforts have resulted in the establishment of numerous educational programs, funding medical research, and supporting initiatives to alleviate poverty and improve access to basic services.

3. What are some criticisms surrounding Carlos Slim?

Despite his impressive achievements, Carlos Slim Helu has faced criticism in several areas, including. allegations of monopolistic practices and anti-competitive behavior within his telecommunications businesses. Additionally, questions have been raised regarding the concentration of wealth and income inequality in Mexico, with Slim being one of the wealthiest individuals in the world.

4. What can we learn from Carlos Slim's success and leadership style?

Carlos Slim's success can be attributed to his strategic thinking, long-term vision, and ability to diversify his investments across different sectors. His leadership style emphasizes discipline, patience, and a focus on long-term value creation. Slim's ability to adapt to changing market conditions and identify emerging opportunities serves as a valuable lesson for aspiring entrepreneurs and business leaders.

5. What is Carlos Slim's net worth?

His current net worth at the time of this writing is estimated at $93.95 billion USD.

Carlos Slim Helu's Success Rules

1. Competition makes you better, always, always makes you better, even if the competitor wins.

2. When you live for others' opinions, you are dead. I don't want to live thinking about how I'll be remembered.

3. Anyone who is not investing now is missing a tremendous opportunity.

5. Any personal crisis — you have to use it to get stronger.

6. "All times are good time for those who know how to work and have the tools to do so."

7. Success is not about doing things well or even very well or being acknowledged by others. It is not an external opinion, but rather an internal status. It is the harmony between the soul and your emotions, which requires love, family, friendship, authenticity and integrity.

8. Most people try to make a better world for our children when what they should be doing is making better children for our world.

9. Well, when I was very young, maybe 12 years, I began to make investments.

10. Poverty isn't solved with donations.

11. Firm and patient optimism always yields its rewards.

12. Staying occupied displaces preoccupation and problems, and when we face our problems, they disappear.

13. I've always said that the better off you are, the more responsibility you have for helping others. Just as I think it's important to run companies well, with a close eye to the bottom

line, I think you have to use your entrepreneurial experience to make corporate philanthropy effective.

14. Money is not a goal. The goal is to make companies grow, develop, be competitive, be in different areas, be efficient to have a great human team inside the company.

15. The truth is, you leave this world with nothing. What you are is a temporary administrator, and you must administer well… the wealth in your care and generate more. The surplus can be used to do many things for people.

16. If you are in business, you are not enjoying, you are working.

17. The only way you finish with poverty is with jobs.

18. In this new wave of technology, you can't do it all yourself, you have to form alliances.

19. It's very important for leaders in business to work to create human capital, a team that has the same sense of purpose and alignment.

20. Work well done is not only a responsibility to yourselves and society; it is also an emotional need.

21. Choose the right employees and then set them loose.

22. When we decide to do something, we do it quickly.

23. In business, you invest when things are not in good shape. When you invest at these times, you take a better position than your competitors. When there is a recession and your competition does not invest, they are giving you the advantage.

24. People need to feel very good about their achievements. They get pride from what they are doing.

25. All businesses make mistakes. The trick is to avoid large ones.

26. One of the big errors people are making right now is thinking that old-style businesses will be obsolete, when actually they will be an important part of this new civilization. Some retail groups are introducing e-commerce and think that the bricks are no longer useful. But they will continue to be important.

27. You cannot have people in your organization who are pessimists. They take you to mediocrity.

28. Courage taught me no matter how bad a crisis gets… any sound investment will eventually pay off.

29. Focus on essentials and try not to get distracted and bogged down by things that don't add value to the bottom line.

30. When we face our problems, they disappear. So learn from failure and let success be the silent incentive.

31. You cannot live without doing something.

32. I learned from my father that you continue to invest and reinvest in your business – including during crises.

33. Anything that has privileges has responsibility and all people [who are] clear about their responsibility have compromise.

34. When you are convinced what to do and what you need to do, it's not hard to do that.

35. Live the present intensely and fully, do not let the past be a burden, and let the future be an incentive. Each person forges his or her own destiny.

36. When there is a crisis, that's when some are interested in getting out and that's when we are interested in getting in.

37. Mistakes are normal and human. Make them small, accept them, correct them, and forget them.

38. Technology is going to transform people's lives and society everywhere in the world. I spend most of my time studying new technologies. My main task is to understand what's going on and try to see where we can fit in.

39. Do not allow negative feelings and emotions to control your mind. Emotional harm does not come from others; it is conceived and developed within ourselves.

40. The biggest things in life are not materials.

41. Life's road is very long, but it is travelled fast.

42. You have to have an international reference of competition. You have to go beyond your home.

43. What is most valuable in life does not cost anything but is very precious.

44. When you give, do not expect to receive; fragrance clings to the hand that gives the rose.

45. If you're in business, you need to understand the environment. You need to have a vision of the future, and you need to know the past.

46. To think that happiness comes from buying things is crazy. That happiness come because you have many material issues – to have 20 cars or 30 cars or the biggest one and 40 watches and – I think that's not happiness.

47. Wealth should be created by investing to create more wealth. Income is the fruit of wealth. If you do not do that, you will not have more income.

48. Distribute a good part of the fruits, not the branches of the tree, and 'reinvest' part of the fruit sees to grow more trees and create wealth.

49. Wealth should be best to create more wealth.

50 If you're in business, you need to understand the environment. You need to have a vision of the future, and you need to know the past.

Slim's top 10 Lessons/Advice for current and future entrepreneur.

1- Be practical and have clear and attainable goals.

2-Invest prodigiously in your business, especially when others aren't investing in theirs, and do so for the long-term.

3- Focus on the essentials and try not to get distracted and bogged down by things that don't add anything of value to the bottom line.

4- Don't try to be and do everything yourself; rather, create alliances and partnerships with others.

5- Be optimistic, and not guided by your fears.

6- Relish competition and understand that it's healthy and will make you and your business stronger.

7- Don't overwork your employees; make sure that they're able to maintain a healthy work/life balance.

8- Choose the right employees and then set them loose.

9- Don't stay local, go global.

10- Finally, acknowledge that as your business grows you may have to install a CEO and several management layers, but try to keep management as flat as possible, so that it stays close to operations because, ultimately, that's where the money is made. (Source: Forbes.com)

Other success rules by Carlos Slim

- Do not allow negative feelings and emotions to control your mind. Emotional harm does not come from others; it is conceived and developed within ourselves. —*Letter to Young People*, Carlosslim.com, June 1994

- All businesses make mistakes. The trick is to avoid large ones. —*Institutional Investor*, June 1, 2007

- **You have to have an international reference of competition. You have to go beyond your home.—No Fear of Failure: Real Stories of How Leaders Deal With Risk and Change, 2011**

- **Mistakes are normal and human. Make them small, accept them, correct them, and forget them. — American University of Beirut, March 18, 2010**

- **Firm and patient optimism always yields its rewards. —Questions and Answers, Carlosslim.com, 2007**

- **I don't believe too much in luck, I believe in circumstances and in work. —George Washington University Global Forum, October 29, 2010**

- **When we face our problems, they disappear. So learn from failure and let success be the silent incentive. - American University of Beirut, March 18, 2010**

Chapter 12

SUCCESS RULES FROM MUKESH AMBANI, INDIA'S ULTRA BILLIONAIRE

Introduction to Mukesh Ambani: His Life and Contributions

Mukesh Ambani, the renowned Indian business tycoon, is a name that resonates with success, innovation, and philanthropy. As the chairman and largest shareholder of Reliance Industries Limited, Ambani has played a pivotal role in transforming India's business landscape. This article delves into the fascinating journey of Mukesh Ambani, exploring his early life and background, his rise to business success, and his significant contributions to various industries. Additionally, we will delve into Ambani's notable philanthropic endeavors, the valuable lessons we can learn from his entrepreneurial journey, his impact on the Indian economy, the challenges he has faced, and his visionary outlook for the future.

1. Early Life and Background

1.1 Early Childhood and Family

Mukesh Ambani, the renowned Indian business tycoon and the chairman and largest shareholder of Reliance Industries Limited, was born on April 19, 1957, in Aden, Yemen. Coming from a family of modest means, Mukesh was raised in a close-knit household that instilled values of perseverance and ambition.

1.2 Education and Influences

Ambani's educational journey was nothing short of remarkable. He pursued a bachelor's degree in chemical engineering from the Institute of Chemical Technology in Mumbai. During his studies, he developed a keen interest in entrepreneurship and innovation, which laid the foundation for his future success.

1.3 Entry into the Business World

After completing his education, Ambani joined Reliance Industries, a company founded by his father, Dhirubhai Ambani. Initially working at the grassroots level, Ambani quickly grasped the nuances of the business and demonstrated his exceptional leadership skills. Little did anyone know that he would soon become a force to be reckoned with in the corporate world.

2. Rise to Business Success

2.1 Expansion of Reliance Industries

Under Ambani's astute guidance, Reliance Industries witnessed unprecedented growth and expansion. He played a pivotal role in transforming the company from a textile-focused enterprise into a conglomerate with interests in petrochemicals, refining, oil, and gas exploration, and telecommunications.

2.2 Diversification into Various Sectors

Recognizing the importance of diversification, Ambani led Reliance Industries into new sectors such as retail, media, and entertainment. Through strategic acquisitions and partnerships, he expanded the company's footprint and solidified its position as a major player in various industries.

2.3 Challenges and Milestones

Ambani's journey to success was not without its share of challenges. He faced intense competition, market fluctuations, and regulatory hurdles. His visionary approach and determination allowed him to overcome these obstacles and achieve remarkable milestones, including leading Reliance Industries to become one of the largest privately-owned companies in India and globally.

3. Ambani's Contributions in the Business World

3.1 Transforming the Indian Telecommunications Industry

Ambani's most notable contribution to the business world came through Reliance Jio Infocomm Limited. Launched in 2016, Jio revolutionized the Indian telecommunications industry by offering affordable data plans and reshaping the digital landscape of the country. This move democratized access to the Internet, empowering millions of Indians and driving digital innovation.

3.2 Impact on the Oil and Gas Sector

Ambani's leadership also had a profound impact on the oil and gas sector, with Reliance Industries emerging as a key player. The company made significant investments in exploration, refining, and petrochemicals, contributing to India's energy security and economic growth.

3.3 Innovations and Technological Advancements

Known for his forward-thinking approach, Ambani spearheaded various innovative initiatives within Reliance Industries. From deploying advanced technologies in manufacturing to fostering research and development, his vision for innovation has helped the company stay ahead of the curve and adapt to changing market dynamics.

4. Philanthropy and Social Initiatives

4.1 Reliance Foundation and its Focus Areas

Ambani's commitment to giving back to society is exemplified through the Reliance Foundation, the philanthropic arm of

Reliance Industries. The foundation focuses on areas such as education, healthcare, rural development, and disaster response, aiming to improve the lives of millions of underprivileged individuals.

4.2 Key Initiatives and Projects

Reliance Foundation has undertaken numerous impactful initiatives, including the establishment of the Sir H.N. Reliance Foundation Hospital, the Indian School of Business in Hyderabad, and the Reliance Institute of Life Sciences. These initiatives reflect Ambani's dedication to creating sustainable solutions and promoting social progress.

4.3 Collaborations and Partnerships

To maximize the impact of its philanthropic efforts, Reliance Foundation collaborates with various organizations, both national and international. By leveraging partnerships, Ambani ensures that the foundation's initiatives reach a wider audience and create a meaningful and lasting difference.

5. Lessons from Mukesh Ambani's Entrepreneurial Journey

5.1 Vision, Leadership, and Strategy

Mukesh Ambani's entrepreneurial journey teaches us the importance of having a clear vision, strong leadership skills, and a well-defined strategy. Ambani's vision to make Reliance Industries a global leader in various sectors, such as petrochemicals, refining, and telecommunications, has guided his decision-making process and provided a roadmap for success. His ability to articulate this vision and inspire his team has been crucial in achieving ambitious goals.

5.2 Adaptability and Risk-taking

Ambani's journey is a testament to the fact that adaptability and risk-taking are essential traits for any entrepreneur. He has demonstrated the ability to adapt to changing market dynamics, technological advancements, and consumer demands. Whether it was diversifying into new sectors or embracing digital transformation, Ambani has shown a willingness to take calculated risks and step out of his comfort zone.

5.3 Importance of Innovation and Disruption

Innovation and disruption are key drivers of success in today's fast-paced world, and Ambani understands this well. From launching Reliance Jio, a game-changer in the Indian telecommunications industry, to investing in cutting-edge technologies like artificial intelligence, Ambani has constantly pushed the boundaries of innovation. His ability to identify emerging trends and disrupt existing market norms has been instrumental in his entrepreneurial journey.

6. Ambani's Impact on the Indian Economy

6.1 Job Creation and Employment Opportunities

Ambani's business ventures have had a significant impact on job creation and employment opportunities in India. Through Reliance Industries, he has established numerous manufacturing units, retail outlets, and telecommunication infrastructure, leading to a substantial increase in employment opportunities across various sectors.

6.2 Contributions to GDP and National Development

Ambani's contributions to the Indian economy cannot be overstated. His investments in diverse sectors have not only contributed to the country's GDP but also played a crucial role in infrastructure development, technological advancements, and overall national progress. His visionary ideas have propelled India's growth trajectory forward.

6.3 Influence on Market Dynamics and Competition

Ambani's presence in various industries has fundamentally reshaped market dynamics and competition. His entry into the telecommunications sector with Reliance Jio sparked a price war, benefiting consumers and forcing existing players to adapt and innovate. Ambani's influence extends beyond his own ventures, as his strategic moves have often set the tone for industry-wide changes.

7. Challenges and Controversies faced by Ambani

7.1 Legal Battles and Regulatory Issues

Like any successful entrepreneur, Ambani has faced his fair share of challenges and legal battles. From disputes over contracts to regulatory issues, he has had to navigate complex legal landscapes. His ability to effectively manage these challenges and emerge stronger speaks to his resilience and determination.

7.2 Criticisms and Allegations

Being a prominent figure in the business world, Ambani has faced criticisms and allegations throughout his career. Critics have questioned his business practices, monopolistic tendencies, and environmental impact. While controversies are inevitable in the public eye, Ambani has consistently focused on addressing concerns and improving his business practices.

7.3 Reputation Management and Response

Ambani's response to controversies and reputation management has been noteworthy. He has taken proactive measures to enhance transparency, corporate governance, and environmental sustainability. Ambani understands the value of maintaining a positive reputation and has consistently worked towards earning the trust and respect of stakeholders.

8. Mukesh Ambani's Vision for the Future

8.1 Sustainability and Green Initiatives

As an advocate for sustainability, Mukesh Ambani is committed to incorporating green initiatives into his business ventures. He recognizes the importance of protecting the environment and believes in building a sustainable future. Ambani's focus on renewable energy, waste reduction, and responsible business practices sets a positive example for others.

8.2 Investments in Technology and Digital Transformation

Ambani's vision for the future heavily relies on investments in technology and digital transformation. His ambitious plan to revolutionize the Indian digital landscape through Reliance Jio has changed the way people connect, communicate, and consume in the country. Ambani continues to invest in emerging technologies, such as artificial intelligence and Internet of Things, to stay ahead of the curve.

8.3 Expansion Plans and Global Outlook

Ambani's vision extends beyond the borders of India. He has ambitious expansion plans and a global outlook for his businesses. Whether it's venturing into new markets or forging strategic partnerships with international companies, Ambani aims to position Reliance Industries as a global powerhouse. His vision for the future includes expanding reach and influence on a global scale.

In conclusion, Mukesh Ambani's biography is a testament to determination, innovation, and a commitment to making a positive impact. From humble beginnings to becoming one of the wealthiest individuals in the world, Ambani's entrepreneurial journey has inspired countless aspiring business leaders. As he continues to spearhead Reliance Industries and contribute to India's economic growth, Ambani's philanthropic efforts further highlight his desire to uplift communities and create a better future. By exploring Ambani's life, business ventures, contributions, philanthropy, and lessons, we gain valuable insights into the remarkable achievements of this business magnate and the enduring legacy he is building.

FAQs

1. What are some of Mukesh Ambani's notable contributions in the business world?

Mukesh Ambani has made significant contributions in various sectors, including transforming the Indian telecommunications industry with the launch of Reliance Jio. He has also played a crucial role in the oil and gas sector, spearheading Reliance's growth and expanding its footprint internationally.

2. How has Mukesh Ambani's philanthropy impacted society?

Mukesh Ambani's philanthropic efforts through Reliance Foundation have focused on areas such as education, healthcare, rural development, and disaster response. His initiatives have made a positive impact by improving access to quality education, healthcare facilities, and empowering marginalized communities.

3. What lessons can we learn from Mukesh Ambani's entrepreneurial journey?

Mukesh Ambani's journey offers valuable lessons for aspiring entrepreneurs, including the importance of vision, leadership, adaptability, and innovation. His ability to navigate challenges, take calculated risks, and embrace technological advancements are inspiring lessons for those looking to succeed in the business world.

4. What is Mukesh Ambani's vision for the future?

Mukesh Ambani envisions a future that embraces sustainability, digital transformation, and global expansion. His focus on green initiatives, investments in technology, and plans for expanding Reliance's presence internationally reflect his vision for driving positive change and growth in the coming years.

5. What is Mukesh Ambani's net worth?

His current net worth at the time of writing (2023) is estimated at $94.62 billion USD.

Mukesh Ambani's Rules for success by Be Courageous

The first lesson is courage. Nobody has ever achieved anything big in business or in any walk of life without courage. Of course, whenever you do anything big you do feel a little scared but you have got to conquer fear to discover the hidden hero within you. With courage, with self-belief and the can-do spirit, you can overcome any adversity.

Find And Solve Problems

The second piece that I learned is that as an entrepreneur, it's very important to find a problem that you want to solve that you are passionate about. I was blessed to have Professor Sharma at the University Department of Chemical Technology (UDCT) (now Institute of Chemical Technology (ICT)).

He would always say I am not going to give you a list of problems and then you can go and work on anything; you find a problem and then I will grade you on the quality of the problem that you find and then I will grade you on the quality of solution that you actually do. So the same rules apply for an entrepreneur, that it's not solving problems, it is first finding problems. Once you find the problem, then you solve it.

Work Hard

Put on your running shoes but remember that personal and professional success is not a sprint but a marathon. We are lucky to be living in a dynamic world where anything is possible but it is important to remember there are no overnight successes you will need to be dedicated, single-minded and there is no substitute to hard work. Also, remember that in this marathon of life is not a rat race, it is important to achieve our goals but not at any cost.

Serve A Higher Purpose

My father (Dhirubhai Ambani) started RIL with $100. When I joined RIL in 1980, the market value of the company was $30 million or $40 million and in 30 years, the opportunities that were provided by this country has enabled us to create wealth for India.

My father was a big believer that any business that has the sole purpose of making money is not worth doing, it must serve a larger societal purpose. RIL raised all its money from capital markets and from individual small shareholders, so we have created a million millionaires just by investing in RIL out of ordinary Indians and that is the process of creating wealth for the country. Once you create opportunity wealth comes.

Accept Failure

Failures are normal. With all the success that one sees, people even in my own case don't see how many times I have failed before I succeed, they are just a step before you succeed. So never get disheartened by failures learn from them but never give up.

Ignore The Naysayers

Keep your headphones on, fill your ears and minds with melodies of optimism, turn out the critics and the cynics, the naysayers - people who say this cannot be done and treat them as noise cancellation. Dance to your own music and take some risks in life because it is often the risk taker who changes the course of history, who innovates, who creates something the world desperately needs and contributes to the well-being of millions of lives.

Feel Empathy

Empathy means caring and sharing with every human being in our organization and the world at large, the more we care the higher we grow as human beings. I understand empathy as 'Dil Ki Daulat', it is the wealth of your heart, the more you spend it on others the wealthier you become.

Make Memories

I think this whole business of making memories. It is such a simple statement but I think it's profound in saying that, and particularly now after Papa, the only thing that we have of him are his memories and they are very dear to us. Nita used to always say this, that every moment is important and that's what life is all about and I understand what she's saying.

Always Be An Optimist

An entrepreneur is always positive, he's an optimist. There are lots of cynics, lots of negative people around but an entrepreneur spreads the positive energy that's really what I have learnt.

Quotes by Mukesh Ambani

- It is important to remember that there are no overnight successes. You will need to be dedicated, single-minded, and there is no substitute to hard work.

- You have to manage money. Particularly with market economies. You may have a great product, but if your bottom line goes bust then that's it.

- My father said if you want to become an entrepreneur you will have to figure things out on your own. Only managers are told what is to be done, not entrepreneurs.

- I think our fundamental belief is that for us growth is a way of life and we have to grow at all times.

- Everybody has equal opportunity and I think that is true for everything.

- Relationships and trust: These are the bedrocks of life.

- Today I see a billion people as a billion potential consumers, an opportunity to generate value for them and to make a return for myself.

- I have turned into a big nature fan as well; I can afford it more today. These childhood influences have shaped me into what I am today.

- "Dance to your own music and take some risks in life, because it is often the risk-taker who changes the course of history... and contribute to the well-being of millions of lives."

- All times are good times for those who know how to work and have the tools to do so.

- It is important to achieve our goals, but not at any cost.

- Mahatma Gandhi's dream of self-reliance can be attained by making use of Internet and technology.

- I am a big believer that technology shapes mankind.

- Broadband and digital services will no longer be a luxury item – a scarce commodity – to be rationed amongst the privileged few.

- My big advantage was to have my father accept me as first-generation.

- My view is to give everyone the space to grow in his own way. When you see restructuring or separations in a family firm, value has almost always been destroyed. This is the first case where value has been enhanced. In that way, it has been a win-win ending.

- Business must serve a larger societal purpose.

- Any business that has the sole purpose of making money is not worth doing.

- Fill your years and minds with melodies of optimism.

- Essentially, whoever is successful, whoever is going to do things that make a difference, is going to be talked about.

- China and India will, separately and together, unleash an explosion of demand.

- All of us, in a sense, struggle continuously all the time, because we never get what we want. The important thing which I've really learned is how do you not give up, because you never succeed in the first attempt.

- Our own childhood was totally different. I guess when you are left on your own, you find your true potential. I remember my father never came to our school even once. Nevertheless, he was hugely interested in our all-round development for which he did some amazing things.

- So, these were the four components of my upbringing – the academic stuff where I was left to myself, Mahendrabhai, my father's passion for creating Reliance, and that last piece was his deep links with the family.

- "A third track running at that time, apart from academics and the fun stuff, was that my father shared with me his passion for business and entrepreneurship form very early on. Even when I was in high school, I used to spend long hours at office on weekend"

Sources: Gracious Quotes, https://graciousquotes.com/mukesh-ambani/ June 28, 2021.

CNBC TV 18,
https://www.cnbctv18.com/entrepreneurship/here-are-9-rules-to-success-from-indias-richest-man-mukesh-ambani-2508201.htm June 28, 2021.

Success Rules from Chris Gardner, a Humble Millionaire

Introduction to Chris Gardner – His Life and Contributions.

To be clear, Chris Gardner is not being included in this important collection because he is a billionaire. He is a humble and generous individual whose resilience, determination, and hard work show that just about anyone can overcome adversities and make something important of their lives. In fact, his life of resilience and grit has been the subject of a popular movie, *The Pursuit of Happyness*. This collection is about the lessons that have helped people from all over the world amass billions in wealth and change their lives and others. We include Chris Gardner herewith as an encouragement to all that you do not have to be a billionaire or even a millionaire to be judged a success. Success is being able to achieve whatever purpose or goals we have set for ourselves. The story of Chris Gardner teaches us that we all can attain reasonable success no matter our current estate. Enjoy the bonus chapter.

This biographical sketch delves into the inspiring life and remarkable achievements of Chris Gardner, exploring his early life, entrepreneurial journey, business success, and key contributions to the industry. We will also examine the valuable life lessons that can be gleaned from Gardner's experiences, his philanthropic endeavors, his ability to overcome adversity, and the lasting impact he has had on future generations. Join us on this insightful journey as we unravel the story of Chris Gardner and draw inspiration from his unwavering pursuit of success and his commitment to making a positive difference in the world.

1. Early Life and Background

1.1 Family Background and Childhood

Chris Gardner's journey to success had humble beginnings. He was born on February 9, 1954, and grew up in a rough neighborhood in Milwaukee, Wisconsin. He faced numerous challenges, including poverty and an absent father figure, however, Gardner's love and admiration for his mother, Bettye Jean, provided him with the strength and inspiration to overcome these obstacles. Her unwavering determination and resilience shaped Gardner's character, motivating him to strive for a better future.

1.2 Education and Early Career

Despite his challenging circumstances, Gardner managed to graduate from high school and went on to pursue higher education at a community college, but he soon found himself drawn to the world of finance. With determination and a hunger for knowledge, Gardner sought opportunities to learn from industry professionals, even if it meant working for free. This determination led him to gain valuable experience and eventually secure a position in the medical supply industry, where he honed his skills in sales and business development.

2. Entrepreneurial Journey and Business Success

2.1 Starting from Scratch: Chris Gardner's Beginnings

Gardner's entrepreneurial journey began when he founded his own brokerage firm, Gardner Rich & Co., starting from scratch and with limited resources. With sheer determination and an infectious enthusiasm, he managed to attract clients, build relationships, and gradually establish a reputable name for himself in the finance industry.

2.2 The Pursuit of Happiness: Gardner's Inspirational Story

Gardner's remarkable journey gained widespread attention when it was portrayed in the critically acclaimed film, *The Pursuit of Happiness*, starring Will Smith. The movie showcased Gardner's unwavering pursuit of happiness and depicted the challenges he faced as a single father striving to provide a better life for his son against all odds. This inspiring story resonated with audiences worldwide, highlighting Gardner's indomitable spirit and never-give-up attitude.

2.3 Building and Scaling Successful Businesses

Throughout his career, Gardner displayed a sharp business acumen, leveraging his knowledge and experience to build and scale successful ventures. Beyond the financial sector, he ventured into philanthropy, real estate, and stock trading. Gardner's ability to adapt, innovate, and seize opportunities allowed him to create wealth and contribute to society in meaningful ways.

3. Key Contributions and Achievements in the Industry

3.1 Innovations and Disruptive Ideas

Gardner's contributions to the finance industry go beyond his personal success. He is known for his innovative thinking and disruptive ideas that challenged traditional norms. Gardner's unconventional approach to investment strategies and his emphasis on ethical practices have left a lasting impact on the industry, inspiring others to think outside the box and prioritize integrity.

3.2 Awards and Recognitions

Gardner's achievements have garnered significant recognition and accolades. He has received numerous awards for his contributions to entrepreneurship, philanthropy, and his commitment to empowering others. These honors reflect the profound impact Gardner has had on individuals and communities, inspiring others to overcome adversity and find their own paths to success.

3.3 Industry Impact and Influence

Gardner's influence extends far beyond his personal achievements. Through his motivational speeches, mentoring programs, and philanthropic endeavors, he has inspired countless individuals to believe in their own potential and pursue their dreams. Gardner's life serves as a powerful reminder that success is not limited by circumstances but is attainable through hard work, determination, and an unwavering belief in oneself.

4. Life Lessons Learned from Chris Gardner's Experiences

4.1 Pursuing Passion and Overcoming Obstacles

From Gardner's journey, we learn the importance of pursuing our passions and interests, even when faced with seemingly insurmountable obstacles. His story demonstrates that relentless determination, combined with unwavering passion, can help us overcome challenges and achieve extraordinary success.

4.2 Embracing Resilience and Perseverance

Gardner's life is a testament to the power of resilience and perseverance. Despite facing setbacks and hardships, he never wavered in his pursuit of a better life for himself and his family. His story inspires us to harness our inner strength and persevere in the face of adversity, knowing that determination and grit can lead us to triumph.

4.3 The Power of Positive Mindset and Self-belief

One of the most significant lessons we can learn from Gardner is the power of a positive mindset and self-belief. Despite the odds stacked against him, he never succumbed to negativity or self-doubt. Instead, he maintained an unwavering belief in his abilities and a positive outlook on life, which ultimately propelled him toward success. Gardner's story reminds us that our mindset and self-belief are crucial in achieving our goals and forging our own paths.

5. Philanthropy and Social Impact Initiatives

5.1 Chris Gardner Foundation: Empowering Underprivileged Individuals

Chris Gardner is not just a successful businessman, but also a compassionate philanthropist. His foundation, aptly named the Chris Gardner Foundation, is dedicated to empowering underprivileged individuals and providing them with opportunities for a better life. Through various initiatives, the foundation focuses on addressing issues such as homelessness, poverty, and lack of access to education. Gardner is a philanthropist who sponsors many charitable organizations, primarily the Cara Program and the Glide Memorial United Methodist Church in San Francisco, where he and his son received desperately needed shelter. He has helped fund a $50 million project in San Francisco that creates low-income housing and opportunities for employment in the area of the city where he was once homeless. As well as offering monetary support, Gardner donates clothing and shoes. He makes himself available for permanent job placement assistance, career counselling and comprehensive job training for the homeless population and at-risk communities in Chicago.

5.2 Supporting Education and Entrepreneurship

One of the key areas of focus for Chris Gardner's philanthropy is education. He strongly believes that education has the power to transform lives and break the cycle of poverty. Through scholarships, mentorship programs, and partnerships with educational institutions, Gardner's foundation supports deserving students in pursuing their dreams.

Additionally, Gardner recognizes the importance of entrepreneurship in creating economic opportunities. His foundation also provides resources and support to aspiring entrepreneurs, particularly those from disadvantaged backgrounds. By fostering an entrepreneurial spirit, Gardner aims not only to empower individuals, but also to contribute to the economic growth of communities.

5.3 Advocacy for Social Change and Equality

Chris Gardner is a firm believer in social change and equality. He uses his platform and influence to advocate for policies that promote social justice and equal opportunities for all. Gardner actively supports organizations and initiatives that work towards addressing systemic issues, such as racial and gender inequality. By raising awareness and lending his voice to important causes, he strives to bring about positive change in society.

6. Overcoming Adversity and Personal Growth

6.1 Insights from Chris Gardner's Personal Challenges

Chris Gardner's life is a testament to the power of resilience and determination. He has faced numerous challenges throughout his journey, including homelessness, financial struggles, and personal hardships. Through these experiences, Gardner has gained invaluable insights into the human spirit, the importance of perseverance, and the ability to overcome even the toughest obstacles.

6.2 Transformative Experiences and Lessons Learned

The adversities Chris Gardner has encountered have not only shaped his character but also provided him with transformative experiences. From sleeping in train stations to becoming a multi-millionaire, Gardner's story is a reminder that with hard work, persistence, and a positive mindset, anyone can overcome adversity and achieve their goals. His life serves as an inspiration to others, reminding them that setbacks are not permanent and that personal growth can come from the most challenging moments.

6.3 Inspiring Others to Overcome Adversity

Chris Gardner's journey from homelessness to success has inspired countless individuals around the world. Through his motivational talks and engagements, he shares his story and imparts wisdom to others facing their own hardships. Gardner encourages people to believe in themselves, chase their dreams, and never give up, no matter how difficult their circumstances may seem. His authenticity and relatability make him a powerful source of inspiration for those seeking to overcome adversity and create a better future for themselves.

7. Legacy and Influence on Future Generations

7.1 Chris Gardner's Enduring Impact

Chris Gardner's impact on society extends far beyond his personal achievements. With his rags-to-riches story and philanthropic efforts, he has become a symbol of hope and empowerment for people from all walks of life. His resilience, determination, and commitment to helping others have left an indelible mark on the hearts and minds of many.

7.2 Inspiring the Next Generation of Entrepreneurs

Gardner's entrepreneurial journey serves as a source of inspiration for aspiring entrepreneurs, especially those facing adversity. By sharing his experiences and lessons learned, he ignites the spark of possibility in others, encouraging them to pursue their entrepreneurial dreams. Gardner's story is a powerful reminder that anyone, regardless of their background, can achieve success and make a difference through entrepreneurship.

7.3 Lessons for Success and Fulfillment in Life

Chris Gardner's life story is filled with valuable lessons for success and fulfillment. From his emphasis on education and lifelong learning to his unwavering belief in the power of perseverance, Gardner's insights resonate with individuals seeking to lead purpose-driven lives. His journey reminds us that success is not only measured by material wealth but also by the positive impact we can have on others and the fulfillment we find in making a difference.

In conclusion, Chris Gardner's biography is a testament to the power of perseverance, resilience, and the unwavering pursuit of one's dreams. From his humble beginnings to his incredible success as an entrepreneur, Gardner has not only achieved remarkable feats but has also made significant contributions to the industry and society as a whole. His life serves as a source of inspiration, teaching us valuable lessons about determination, embracing challenges, and the importance of giving back. Through his philanthropy and advocacy, Gardner continues to make a positive impact on the lives of others. Gardner's remarkable journey from adversity to success serves as an inspiration to us all to chase our own dreams, overcome obstacles, and leave a lasting legacy that uplifts and empowers others. His unwavering determination, resilience, and entrepreneurial spirit are not only reflected in his achievements but have left a lasting impact on individuals worldwide. Gardner's story teaches us valuable life lessons about pursuing our passions, overcoming obstacles, and embracing a positive mindset, reminding us that greatness can be achieved by anyone with the right mindset and unwavering determination.

FAQs

1. What are some of Chris Gardner's notable business ventures?

Chris Gardner is known for his successful ventures in the stock brokerage industry. One of his notable business endeavors was founding the brokerage firm Gardner Rich & Co., which specialized in the execution of futures contracts. He also had a substantial impact as a motivational speaker and author, sharing his insights and experiences to inspire others.

2. How did Chris Gardner overcome adversity on his path to success?

Chris Gardner faced numerous challenges throughout his life, including homelessness and financial struggles. However, he persevered through sheer determination and unwavering self-belief. Gardner worked tirelessly to secure a position as a stockbroker while facing immense personal hardships, ultimately proving that with resilience and tenacity, anyone can overcome adversity.

3. What philanthropic initiatives is Chris Gardner involved in?

Chris Gardner is deeply committed to philanthropy and social impact. He established the Chris Gardner Foundation, which focuses on empowering disadvantaged individuals by providing access to education, job training, and support services. Additionally, Gardner actively supports various organizations dedicated to addressing homelessness, poverty, and educational inequality.

4. How has Chris Gardner's story inspired others?

Chris Gardner's story has inspired countless individuals around the world. His journey from homelessness to success serves as a powerful reminder that no dream is too big to pursue. Through his motivational speeches and books, Gardner encourages others to embrace their passions, overcome obstacles, and create a brighter future for themselves.

5. What is Chris Gardner's net worth?

His net worth is not fully known but it is generally estimated at about $70 million to $100 million, as of the time of this writing.

Chris Gardner's Success Rules

- Decide to be world-class: Strive to be the best you can be in what you are doing and be persistent.

- Have self-worth: Never confuse your net worth with your self-worth. Your net worth can fluctuate up and down but your self-worth should not. Who you are and your values, should never be negotiable, compromised, and [you] should never settle.

- Keep your team motivated: How do you motivate key employees? You have to respect them, let them grow and trust them. Then, you have to leave them alone. You also have to show them how they could make more money than they have ever made in their lives. By helping them believe in themselves, by igniting passion and determination, you can help them reach an incredible amount of personal development leading to success.

- Change is necessary: Change is scary. With status quo, you know what you've got. With change, you don't know what you might end up with. There are, however, two true things about change: it is absolutely necessary for personal growth and it's going to happen. Either you pick the time to instigate change in your life, or time and change will pick you.

- Baby steps count: Baby steps count as long as you're going forward. Keep going forward and one day those added baby steps may surprise you.

- Follow your passion: Life is short. What are you going to do with the rest of your life? If you are doing something that you are not fully committed to, if you are doing something you are not passionate about, you are compromising yourself every day.

- Do whatever it takes: If you have a goal, if you have a dream, go after it. Don't let anything stand in your way. You may get tired, you may get frustrated, you may get discouraged, but do whatever it takes to keep going toward your goals.

- Start where you are: Create an opportunity where your skills and talents can be transferable. Find something that you are so passionate about that you cannot wait for the sun to come up so you can continue working on it. Where do you start? Start from where you are and take those necessary steps to help you live your passion.

Inspirational Success Quotes

- I was homeless but I wasn't hopeless. I knew a better day was coming.

- Don't ever let someone tell you, you can't do something. Not even me.

- You got a dream you got to protect it.

- People can't do something themselves; they want to tell you, you can't do it.

- The secret to success: find something you love to do so much, you can't wait for the sun to rise to do it all over again.

- The world is your oyster. It's up to you to find the pearls.

- It can be done, but you have to make it happen.

- If you believe you can do it, you will.

- Do something that makes you happy and makes you feel good about yourself.

- You want something, go get it. Period.

- There is no plan B for passion.

- Start where you are.

- It's okay to fail; it's not okay to quit.

- Others may question your credentials, your papers, your degrees. Others may look for all kinds of ways to diminish your worth. But what is inside you no one can take from you or tarnish.

- Claim ownership of your dreams.

- If you don't take the necessary steps to make them happen, dreams are just mirages that mess with your head.

- I am strong because I've been weak. I am fearless because I've been afraid. I am wise because I've been foolish.

- Walk the walk and go forward all the time.

- You can only depend on yourself. The cavalry ain't coming.

- You have to be bold.

- Every finish line is the beginning of a new race.

- The most inspiring leaders are not those who do their job, but those who pursue a calling.

- I hold one thing dearer than all else: my commitment to my son

- Ready or not, tell yourself to jump.

- Strong people stand up for themselves; the strongest people stand up for others.

- This part of my life, this little part is called happiness.

- Do something that you love.

- The future was uncertain, absolutely, and there were many hurdles, twists, and turns to come, but as long as I kept moving forward, one foot in front of the other, the voices of fear and shame, the messages from those who wanted me to believe that I wasn't good enough, would be stilled.

- Your struggle is not an excuse, it's your ammunition.

- Always, always pursue happiness.

- One of the things young people always ask me about is what is the secret to success. The secret is there is no secret. It's the basics. Blocking and tackling.

- (The movie) is the story of my life, but it's not about me. It's about anybody who ever dreamed big and had someone tell them, 'No, you can't do it.' You can.

- You know how mountains get moved? Everyone who can move a couple, move a couple. Those who can move rocks, move rocks. Those who can move boulders, move boulders. That's how mountains get moved. If every one of us did everything we could, I believe we would be in a different world.

- Make your vision larger than yourself.

- Then again, what seems like nothing in the eyes of the world, when properly valued and put to use, can be among the greatest riches.

- The balance in your life is more important than the balance in your checking account.

- Without that sense of self, no amount of paper, no pedigree, and no credentials can make you legit. No matter what, you have to feel legit inside first.

- As busy as I am wherever I am, I try to get out and walk the streets, to remember how far I've come and appreciate every baby step of the way.

- It's your responsibility to pursue what matters.

- Still a dreamer, yet more of a realist than ever before, I knew this was my time to sail. On the horizon I saw the shining future, as before. The difference now was that I felt the wind at my back. I was ready.

- Though my mom had too many of her own dreams denied, deferred and destroyed, she instilled in me that I could have dreams. And not just have dreams but I had a responsibility to make them a reality. My mom taught me from a very early age that I could do anything I wanted to do.

- Do something that makes you feel your work is significant and meaningful.

- No matter how much money is involved or no matter how easy it is for you to do, if you're not happy, you are nothing more than a slave to your talent and money.

- Wealth can also be that attitude of gratitude with which we remind ourselves every day to count our blessings.

- Find something that you love. Something that gets you so excited you can't wait to get out of bed in the morning. Forget about money. Be happy.

Source: Lead Grow Develop,
https://leadgrowdevelop.com/chris-gardners-top-ten-rules-for-success/ June 27, 2021.

About Kharis Publishing:

Kharis Publishing, an imprint of Kharis Media LLC, is a leading Christian and inspirational book publisher based in Aurora, Chicago metropolitan area, Illinois. Kharis' dual mission is to give voice to under-represented writers (including women and first-time authors) and equip orphans in developing countries with literacy tools. That is why, for each book sold, the publisher channels some of the proceeds into providing books and computers for orphanages in developing countries so that these kids may learn to read, dream, and grow. For a limited time, Kharis Publishing is accepting unsolicited queries for nonfiction (Christian, self-help, memoirs, business, health and wellness) from qualified leaders, professionals, pastors, and ministers.

Learn more at: https://kharispublishing.com/

www.ingramcontent.com/pod-product-compliance
Lightning Source LLC
Chambersburg PA
CBHW070032100426
42740CB00013B/2670